THE SOCIAL HISTORY OF EDUCATION

GENERAL EDITOR : VICTOR E. NEUBURG

First Series — No. 4

"LIGHT, MORE LIGHT!"

THE SOCIAL HISTORY OF EDUCATION
GENERAL EDITOR: VICTOR E. NEUBURG

First Series of Eight Titles

No. 1. Edward Baines

The Social, Educational, and Religious State of the Manufacturing Districts; with Statistical Returns of the Means of Education and Religious Instruction in the Manufacturing Districts of Yorkshire, Lancashire, and Cheshire; in Two Letters to the Right Hon. Lord Wharncliffe, on Sir Jas. Graham's Factory Education Bill; also the objectives to the Amended Bill   (2nd ed. 1843).

No. 2 Mary Carpenter

Reformatory Schools, for the Children of the Perishing and Dangerous classes, and for Juvenile Offenders   (1851).

No. 3. Central Society of Education

First, Second and Third Publications (1837, 1838, 1839). Three Volumes.

No. 4. James Hole

"Light, more Light!" On the present State of Education amongst the Working Classes of Leeds, and How it Can Best be improved   (1860).

No. 5. J. W. Hudson

The History of Adult Education, in which is comprised a full and complete history of the mechanics' and literary institutions, Anthenaeums, philosophical mental and christian improvement societies, literary unions, schools of design etc., of Great Britain, Ireland, America etc.   (1851).

No. 6. Sir James Kay Shuttleworth

Memorandum on Popular Education   (1868).

No. 7. C. J. Montague

Sixty Years in Waifdom or, The Ragged School Movement in English History with a Preface by the Most Noble the Marquis of Northampton   (1904).

No. 8. Thomas Pole

A History of the Origin and Progress of Adult Schools; with An Account of some of the beneficial Effects already Produced on the Moral Character of the Labouring Poor   (1814).

"LIGHT, MORE LIGHT!"

ON THE

PRESENT STATE OF EDUCATION

AMONGST THE

WORKING CLASSES OF LEEDS

JAMES HOLE

AUGUSTUS M. KELLEY PUBLISHERS
New York 1969

Published by
WOBURN BOOKS LIMITED
9 RUSSELL CHAMBERS, BURY PLACE, LONDON WC1

Published in the United States by
Augustus M. Kelley, Publishers
New York, New York 10010

First edition   1860
New impression   1969

Printed in Holland by
N.V. Grafische Industrie Haarlem

NEW INTRODUCTION

Beyond the barest outline of his career, very little is known of James Hole's private life. He was born in London in 1820, and seems to have spent part of his youth in Manchester, where he was a member of the Mechanics' Institute. Early in the 1840s he came to Leeds, where for the next twenty-five years or so he was a prominent figure in various reform movements, besides writing several books and contributing to a number of journals on topics relating to the improvement of working class life in Leeds and elsewhere. In 1867 he moved to London where he died in 1895.

Amongst the subjects with which he was concerned were co-operative ventures, housing and above all, education, which he regarded not as a privilege to be bestowed at will upon working men, but as their fundamental right. His abiding interest in the problems of adult education is attested by the fact that for twenty years he was Honorary Secretary of the Yorkshire Union of Mechanics' Institutes. Almost certainly because of his preoccupation with this movement, Hole felt himself obliged to consider the whole question of general education and how in particular a national system could best be provided. He held that the voluntary system was inadequate, and favoured an extension of government finance at both local and central level, though with some reservations.

This book was a prize essay, the money for which had been left to Leeds Mechanics' Institute by the Tory-Radical Vicar of Leeds, Dr. Hook, when he left the city in 1859. It was laid down that the essay should be "on some subject connected with the social advancement of the working classes", the title being chosen by the office holders of the Mechanics' Institute, and the judges were to be the Vicar of Leeds, the Headmaster of the Grammar School and the President of the Institute.

Hole elected not to write about educational policy, but rather to survey the educational agencies which were at work in Leeds, and he tackled this subject with the thoroughness which was a characteristic feature of all his work. He considers the kind of school - day, evening, Sunday, secondary; criminal and pauper education, the School of Art, Mechanics' Institutes and other local educational endeavours. Moreover he discusses the role played by popular literature, cheap concerts and savings banks in the process of "social education". Such a widely ranging concept of education gives this book an unusual value; it provides a detailed picture of precisely what education was available to the working class in Leeds over one hundred years ago.

In the words of a contemporary reviewer in the "Working Men's College Magazine", published in London:

> "The little book to which these last words of Goethe as a title or motto is a statistical account of the present state of education amongst the working classes of Leeds. It is interesting as giving an estimate of the sum total of educational endeavour in a place which may be taken as a specimen (rather a favourable one perhaps) of our great provincial towns."

Repeatedly Hole stresses the great benefits of the grants-in-aid system and shows how a small sum can be made to go a long way. He points out too that such means of financing schools preserve the freedom of religious bodies to act or not to act in educational matters. It is somewhat surprising that Hole does not advocate a thoroughgoing scheme for state education. This is perhaps due to the fact that in all his writings he tended to underline the collective rather than the individual element in social problems, and seems also, like other reformers, to mistrust Government intervention. It was not indeed until two years before his death that he published NATIONAL RAILWAYS, in which he argued cogently for a state-run railway system.

As a social thinker, James Hole has received less than his due, and this edition of LIGHT, MORE LIGHT! is not only of considerable intrinsic interest, but shows that he came near to regarding education as the means by which the working class could help to change society.

V. E. N.
October 1968

Bibliographical Note:

The best account of James Hole and his work is to be found in the following pamphlet, which was invaluable in the preparation of the foregoing;

J. F. C. Harrison: SOCIAL REFORM IN VICTORIAN LEEDS. THE WORK OF JAMES HOLE, 1820-1895.
Thoresby Society Monography No. 3: 1954.

"*Light, more Light!*"

ON THE

PRESENT STATE OF EDUCATION

AMONGST THE

𝔚𝔬𝔯𝔨𝔦𝔫𝔤 𝔆𝔩𝔞𝔰𝔰𝔢𝔰 𝔬𝔣 𝔏𝔢𝔢𝔡𝔰,

AND

HOW IT CAN BEST BE IMPROVED.

BY

JAMES HOLE,

Hon. Sec of the Yorkshire Union of Mechanics' Institutes.

LONDON:

LONGMAN, GREEN, LONGMAN, AND ROBERTS.

1860.

. . . A thousand cheerful omens give
Hope of yet happier days, whose dawn is nigh.
He who has tamed the elements, shall not live
The slave of his own passions; he whose eye
Unwinds the eternal dances of the sky,
And in the abyss of brightness dares to span
The sun's broad circle, rising yet more high,
In God's magnificent work His will shall scan,
And love and peace shall make their paradise with man.

PREFACE.

A few words are necessary to explain the circumstances under which the following Essay is submitted to the public.

Before the Dean of Chichester left Leeds, amongst other marks of his attachment to the place where he had laboured so successfully and so long, he presented £50 to the Leeds Mechanics' Institute, £10 of this sum to be expended in a prize for the best Essay on some subject connected with the social advancement of the working classes; the subject to be chosen by the President, the Vice-presidents, and the Secretaries; and the prize to be adjudged by the Vicar of Leeds, the Head Master of the Grammar School, and the President for the time being of the Institution.

Several Essays were written in competition for this prize, all exhibiting merit and considerable research; the adjudicators, however, considered that upon the whole the following Essay contained a greater variety of important statistical information, and adhered more closely to the subject, than any of the others.

Without pledging themselves, therefore, to entire agreement with all the author's views, they adjudged the prize to the Essay bearing the motto: "More Light, more Light!" which is now presented to the public with the writer's name attached, of which the adjudicators were ignorant.

JAMES ATLAY, D.D., VICAR.

ALFRED BARRY, B.D.,
Head Master of the Leeds Grammar School;

JNO. HOPE SHAW,
President of the Leeds Mechanics' Institute.

Leeds, 23rd August, 1860.

CONTENTS.

CHAPTER I.

CHAPTER II.

CHAPTER III.

CHAPTER IV.

CHAPTER V.

SECONDARY INSTRUCTION.

CHAPTER VI.

EDUCATION IN LEEDS.

CHAPTER I.

INTRODUCTION.

AN enquiry into the state of Education in Leeds
has both a special and a general interest.

It must be of consequence to every citizen of our
busy and thriving community, to know how we
stand in this, one of the highest and most important elements affecting our social condition.
Next to a man's own condition and that of his
family, the welfare of the citizens among whom his
lot is cast, who come in contact with him in so
many relations,—as friends, neighbours, or cus-
tomers, or with whom at least he is associated as a
member of the same municipal and political body,—
must surely be of the greatest concern.

Then, again, although our enquiry is a local one,
yet what is true of Leeds holds good, to a considerable extent, of other parts of the country, especially

the large towns; and therefore the principles and facts deducible from the state of Leeds, have an almost national application. Day Schools, Sunday Schools, Evening Schools, Mechanics' Institutions, Reformatories, Ragged Schools, and the necessities and evils that give rise to these agencies, are pretty much the same in all the chief centres of population.

In Leeds, as in all the large seats of industry, there is much to rejoice at in the state of education among the labouring classes, but yet too much to mourn over. On the one hand, thanks to the great exertions which have been made on behalf of popular education during the last few years,—thanks, too, to the wonderful development and organization of manufacturing industry, to free institutions, and especially to a free press and public meetings,—to libraries, museums, and exhibitions,—to cheap railway trips, and numerous other ameliorative social agencies,—the working classes have been, and still are, undergoing a rapid improvement. But, on the other hand, if the state of information be closely scrutinized, it will be found that large masses are yet steeped in the grossest ignorance. The history of their own country, not to speak of that of other

portions of the human race, are entirely unknown
to them. The ordinary facts of physical science,
the daily phenomena of life, and the physical laws
operating in the beautiful world around them, and
in the worlds of the infinite space beyond, are
utterly unappreciated. The important laws of
health, and the conditions of social wellbeing, are
very imperfectly understood. A gross sensuality,
born of ignorance and fostered by hosts of demoralizing agencies, degrades the life of numbers to a
state of mere animalism, deficient alike in moral
principle and aspiration.

Occasionally, facts transpire which show that the
lowest superstitions can flourish among us ; nay,
exist side by side, with a most remarkable increase
in the provision for education.

If these statements be true, and that they are so
every observer's experience proves, it shows that
while much has been done for education, still more
requires to be done. The questions of pressing
urgency are these :—What are the existing means
of popular education? What are their deficiencies?
And how may these be best supplied ?

The provision for the education of the labouring
classes naturally divides itself into two heads,—

Juvenile and Adult Instruction. The former includes

> DAY SCHOOLS,
> SUNDAY SCHOOLS,
> EVENING SCHOOLS;

the latter, MECHANICS' and similar INSTITUTES. In addition to these agencies, some others which are intimately connected with the progress of education, either as causes or effects, will be briefly considered.

CHAPTER II.

DAY SCHOOLS.

It is almost impossible, without the aid of State authority, to obtain reliable statistics of Day School instruction. The Census of 1851 gave most important information upon this point, and it is much to be regretted that the Census of 1861 will not include educational statistics. The evidence on the state of education now being collected by the Royal Commission, though valuable, will necessarily be much less complete than a Census return, and will neither afford proper means of comparing the progress of education during the past ten years, nor show the full extent of existing deficiencies. So far as ascertaining the increase of schools and pupils in Leeds, it is a fortunate circumstance that, in 1839, complete Returns were obtained by Mr. Robert Baker, for the Leeds Town Council.* The

---

* These valuable returns included the occupations, houses, number of public-houses, and beerhouses, and other important information. They have never been printed, but have been kindly lent by Mr. Baker for use in this paper.

following table will shew the comparison between
the two periods:—

TOWNSHIP, 1839.—MR. BAKER'S TABLES.

SCHOOLS.	PUPILS.		TOTAL.	POPULATION.	Proportion of Scholars to Population.	
	Male.	Female.			Per cent.	Or 1 in
154	3,718	3,041	6,759	82,121	8.23	12.15

BOROUGH, 1851.—CENSUS RETURN.

SCHOOLS.	PUPILS.		TOTAL.	POPULATION.	Proportion of Scholars to Population.	
	Male.	Female.			Per cent.	Or 1 in
371	11,986	9,848	21,834	172,270	12.67	7.89

Assuming, as we may fairly do, that the proportion of schools in the township and the borough are
about the same, the increase of scholars in Leeds, in
the twelve years between 1839 and 1851, would be
about four-and-a-half per cent. The mere increase
in the numbers of scholars was not very remarkable.
The greatest improvement was in the *quality* of the
schools, and of the instruction given therein. A
large number of superior schools were built, and the

assistance offered by the Committee of Council on
Education, in grants, trained teachers, and pupil
teachers, was largely taken advantage of. Much
the greater proportion of these schools have been
those of the Church of England. We have not
space to discuss the cause of this preponderance;
but in justice to the clergy (a justice not often con-
ceded to them in educational discussions), it must
be admitted that they are more active originators
of schools, and take a greater interest in promoting
their success, than almost any other portion of the
community. Had, indeed, the other denominations
but availed themselves of the Government aid to
anything like a proportionate extent, we should,
as regards the supply of schools, have hardly anything to complain of. Even as it is, whatever
deficiency exists in the extent of Day School
instruction, arises not so much from want of
more schools, as of a fuller use of the existing ones.
Leeds is well supplied with schools, though in one
or two districts an additional school would be useful.
The following table, extracted from the "Returns
of the School Inspectors in 1853," shows how
largely the proportion of schools in connexion with
the Committee of Council on Education are Church

Schools, and also, that at that time the school accommodation was almost double that required for the number of pupils in attendance.

	SCHOOLS.	NUMBER OF SCHOLARS.		CHARACTER OF SCHOOL.	
		That building will hold, allowing 8 square feet to each Scholar.	In average Attendance.	Satisfactory.	Indifferent.
Church of England	30	9,958	5,500	19	11
British Schools .	3	791	305	1	
Wesleyan . . .	4	1,335	576	2	
Roman Catholic .	1	200	148	1	
	38	12,284	6,529		

The previous comparison of 1839 and 1851, shows the increase in Day Schools of *all* descriptions.

But, as this enquiry is limited to children of the labouring classes, we have endeavoured to estimate the number of scholars of this class. We exclude the Grammar Schools, and many private schools, because all these are intended either for the middle classes, or those between the middle and the artizan class. For all other schools it may be safely assumed that, with few exceptions (which have also been included as far as practicable), the schools which receive the Parliamentary Grant and are liable to Inspection, constitute almost the entire provision for Day Schools for the children of the labouring classes. The quality of these schools is so superior, that, except a few dame schools not worth notice, *private* schools for this class of pupils have almost ceased. It is, therefore, a comparison of the increase in the pupils of these schools, that will best indicate the progress made in the extension of popular education. According to the Inspectors' reports, and other sources of information, there are, in schools for the children of the *labouring classes*, in Leeds, at the present time, (May, 1860,)

	CHILDREN.
In Public Schools, under Inspection . .	10,017
„ „ not under Inspection .	1,994
„ Private Day Schools	2,454
	14,465

The following table shows how rapid has been the increase of scholars in Inspected schools during the last seven years.

Pupils in Schools under Inspection, in the Borough of Leeds, in 1853 *and* 1860.

Date.	Number of Pupils in Schools under Inspection.	Proportion of Scholars to Population.	
		Per cent.	Or 1·in
1853	6,529	3.79	26
1860	10,017	5.22	19

Valuable as the Parliamentary Grant has been, and we are not at all disposed to underrate its importance, we still think that an exaggerated idea has been entertained as to its relative extent.* We have taken from the "Minutes" the grants to every school in Leeds, from the first, and find the amount, in itself, very small; but compared with the results achieved by its aid, in the stimulus it has given to popular education, we venture to say that never was

---

* Only recently, Mr. Gladstone stated the Education Grants to amount to £1,700,000 per year, and the statement was paraded in some newspapers opposed to the grants for schools, as if the whole amount was for the purpose. The truth is, that the last year's grant, and the largest, was only £723,115, and the *total* amount since the establishment of the Government Grants to schools, from 1839 to 31st December, 1859, has been only £4,378,183, about one-sixteenth of the national taxation for a single year. It is most unfair to include grants for other national objects, (no doubt important ones,) as if they were grants for the National School system, and then to argue from such erroneous data.

the same amount of money so well expended. The following is the total amount of Parliamentary Grants to schools in the borough of Leeds, from the the commencement of such aid in 1836, to 1859, inclusive :—

	£.	s.	d.
Grants for building, enlargement, improvement, or fixtures . . .	16,232	14	4
Grants for apparatus, books, maps, and diagrams	500	4	3
Grants to certificated teachers . .	5,739	17	6
Grants for assistant teachers . . .	790	19	2
Grants to pupil teachers, and gratuities to masters and mistresses	23,867	10	0
Capitation Grants	2,295	15	5
Total,	£49,427	0	8

To the above £49,427 0s. 8d., must be added the voluntary contributions of the friends of education, upon condition of which the grants could alone have been obtained, and which may be estimated at nearly twice as much more. Some idea of the character of the schools of twenty years ago, may be drawn from the following facts, taken from

Mr. Baker's report before alluded to. Out of the 154 schools, 42 were kept by male, and 112 by female teachers. At a time when there were no grants from the Committee of Council on Education, and scarcely any public subscriptions in aid, the fees were :—

PER WEEK.

In 82 schools, under . . . . 3d.

" 27 " between . . . . 3d. and 4d.

" 45 " . . . . 6d. and above.

——
154
——

It is not surprising to learn that, of the 154 schools, writing and accounts were *not* taught in eighty, or more than half of them. The report remarked : " Many of those schools where the charge is under threepence a week, bear the character of dame schools only,—and are, in fact, more nurseries for keeping children out of harm's way during the employment of the mother, than really for the purposes of education. In very few is anything taught beyond the elements of the English language, by teachers more fitted themselves to be scholars than teachers, and rarely, if ever, upon a system upon proper principles. The Factory Schools also bear this character, with the exception of three or

four, and, as in the others, the education bestowed
is of the most meagre description,—places for men
and women, rather than men and women for places
of so highly an important character."

Contrasted with the former state of Day Schools,
their present condition is admirable. Not to speak
of the great improvement in the Grammar School,
and the private schools for the middle classes, which
are excluded from the present enquiry, how much
has been done in the improvement of the schools
for children of the labouring classes, and which is
almost entirely due to the assistance of the Committee of Council on Education. In almost every
part of the borough, large and commodious schools
have been erected, trained teachers have been supplied, comparative efficiency has been introduced
into the system of juvenile education, and, by means
of Inspection, a guarantee is afforded, not only that
the money at present spent is properly applied,
but that the seeds of further progress shall be
allowed to take root as fast as practicable. It is
not contended that the system is perfect; no doubt
that a great injustice is done to those poorer districts
which cannot get the Government Grant, because
they cannot offer the proper quota of voluntary

support; but, taken as a whole, it is questionable if any other system could have effected the same amount of good at so small a cost. It has kept primary instruction in the hands of the best friends of education, and has freed it from the risks which it might have run from political or municipal squabbles. It has left full freedom of action, or inaction, to the various religious bodies, who, whether for good or ill, have assumed the duty of taking charge of the education of the people. Without superseding or weakening the sense of responsibility which parents should feel in the education of their children, it has utilized their contributions, and given them the best practicable system at the smallest possible cost. The only matter of regret is, that influential religious denominations, distinguished by intelligence, wealth, and social influence, and by no means indifferent to the spread of education, have held aloof on grounds as mistaken as they are conscientious, and thus seriously curtailed the extent and advantages which education would have derived from their co-operation.*

---

* Mr. HARRY CHESTER thus describes the schools of twenty years ago:—

" When the Committee of Council on Education was first created, in

The great drawback to efficiency of the schools is the early age at which children are withdrawn from them to go to work. The following table shows the early period when children leave school,

---

1839, so little attention had been given to the planning of schools, that they were commonly erected by the village bricklayer and carpenter, by rule of thumb, without any plans at all. The organisation of schools had been little studied. A minimum education was given at a minimum cost. Babies, of eight and ten years old, were set to teach other babies of the same age; the national infantry were still drawn up in Dr. Bell's hollow squares; writing desks were few, scanty, and fixed to the walls; and Dr. Bell's original plan of teaching poor children to write, by marking out letters with their fingers in shallow troughs of sand, had not long been abandoned. Of apparatus there was little but a few slates; of maps there was perhaps one, a meagre map of Palestine; of books there were scarcely any but the Holy Bible. In the Holy Bible, used as a primer, little children were drilled in spelling and reading; and their arithmetic was too often drawn from the same source. When the New Zealander takes up his proper position upon London Bridge, he will scarcely be able to credit the statement—and yet it is true—that, in the 19th century, a manual of arithmetic was published by a learned divine, an excellent person, for the use of National Schools, in which, in order to give to children a reverence for sacred things, the sums set were drawn from historical statements of numbers in the Holy Scriptures! 'There were twelve patriarchs, twelve apostles, and four evangelists; add the patriarchs and evangelists together; subtract the apostles, what is the remainder?' 'Solomon had so many wives and so many concubines; add the concubines to the wives, and state the result.'

"The buildings were low, thin, dingy, ill-drained, often without means of warming, often without proper conveniences; with no furniture but a teacher's desk, a few rickety forms, a rod, a cane, and a fool's-cap; the floors were almost invariably of brick,— the worst kind of floor, as it is tenacious of moisture, cold to the feet, easily abraded into red dust, and soon worn into holes. There were rarely any porches or lobbies for the

and the inducement, in the shape of wages, that
leads to this result.*

Wages, &c., of Children leaving School.

SCHOOL.	Average Age at which the last 100 have left,	Whole School-time in this or any School,	Per centage who have been in Infants' School,	Average Rate of Wages obtained at leaving School,
	Years.	Years.		
St. George's . .	10.42	6.08	61.5	4s. to 5s.
St Paul's . . .	9.48	5.38	87.	3s. ,, 5s.
St. Andrew's . .	9.25	4.07	68.	3s. ,, 6s.
Quarry-Hill . .	8.22	4.25	54.	4s. ,, 5s.
Benley . . .	8.28	3.68	56.	3s. ,, 6s.
Messrs. Marshall's	11.05	6.25	47.	3s. ,, 4s.
St. Mark's . .	9.65	4.91	0.	2s. ,, 4s.
Kirkstall . . .	7.52	2.33	23.	3s. ,, 6s.
St. Matthew's .	11.03	5.02	53.	3s. ,, 4s.
St. Philip's . .	9.31	4.88	70.	4s.
Average .	9.59	4.73	51.75	3/2 to 5s.

* *Minutes,* 1857 and 1858, page 295. *Report of the Rev. F. Watkins.*

caps and cloaks of the children. If there were a house for the teacher, it
was seldom such a house as a teacher at the present day would like to in-
habit. Now, however, all this is improved."—*Address on National
Education.*

The second column represents the length of school instruction as about four years and nine months, but the third column leads to the conclusion that a considerable portion of even that short time must have been spent in the Infant School.

According to the last Report of the Rev. F. Watkins, the children at school in 1859 in Yorkshire (and the case of Leeds is, for all practical purposes, the same), are of the following ages :—

Under 7 years of age, . . . 38.0 per cent.
„ 10 „ . . . 72.5
Above 10 „ . . . 27.5

That is, 38 out of every hundred are under seven years ; 72 out of each hundred are under ten ; and only 27 out of the hundred are over the age of ten. Mr. Watkins points out, that so far from mending, the state of matters has been deteriorating for many years past.* In fact, as the schools have improved, the standard school age has lowered, or as it is well expressed, " the better a school is, the shorter time do children of the working class stay in it. Nearly nine-tenths of the children of the working classes stay at school only about three years, and are then sent out to their work in life."

---

* *Minutes*, 1859-60, page 33.

The attendance at schools is thus stated :—*

In school less than 1 year . . . 42.21 per cent.†

Who have been 1 year . . . 23.15 „

„ „ 2 years . . . 15.38 „

„ „ 3 „ . . . 9.86 „

„ „ 4 „ . . . 4.97 „

„ „ 5 „ and upwards 4.44 „

In consequence of this state of things, acquisitions made at so early a period cannot possibly leave much lasting impression. The results upon the intellect and character of the pupil, are by no means equal to what they ought to be. For example, out of 1,946 marriages in the Leeds and Hunslet districts in 1857, there were 478 men, or more than 25 per cent.,—870 women, or 45 per cent., who signed the marriage register with marks. In "Medical Notes on the Militia," Mr. J. Ingham Ikin, of Leeds, states, that of the 2,000 recruits first inspected at the commencement of 1854, 950 could neither write nor read ! Of the recruits for regiments of the line

---

* *Minutes*, 1859-60, page 34.

† As Mr. Watkins remarks, the above table shows only the stay of the children at *one* school. The total school-stay is longer than stated in the above returns, owing to the children going from one school to another; but, on the other hand, the change of school is very unfavourable to their improvement.

inspected in 1857, 205 out of 300 could neither write nor read.

The Rev. J. P. Norris states, as the result of enquiries in all the schools of the district under his Inspection, that "three children out of four leave school with only such a smattering of education as they may have picked up in the lower classes ; that the more advanced lessons in elementary schools,— lessons in geography, in grammar, in English history, in the higher parts of arithmetic, in drawing, in cutting out and fixing for needlework, —are brought within the reach of only a fourth part of the scholars." "Such facts," he adds, " will doubtless go far to console those who are alarmed lest there be none left, ere long, to hew wood and draw water. It will reassure them to know, on the authority of an Inspector of schools, that three-fourths of our children still leave school without having learned who Queen Victoria's predecessor was, or what river flows by London. * * Neither *intellectually nor morally can our schools be held responsible for three-fourths of the children who have nominally passed through them.*"*

This transitory instruction is much more detrimental to the children of the working classes than to those of the middle ranks, because the latter have not only a considerably longer attendance at the Day School than those of the working classes, but their acquisitions are kept up (in part at least) by their avocations as merchants, shopkeepers, and clerks, as well as by their intercourse with the educated world by means of books, newspapers, and general literature. The children of the working class, on the other hand, rarely preserve that skill in reading and writing which makes the practice of those arts easy or agreeable pursuits for their own sake ; and manual labour, to which they are called so much too early, does not stimulate the exercise of the intellectual faculties.

We know not who can justly be called gainers by this early transference of the child from the school to the factory. Is it the child ? His welfare should be indeed the principal element in the question, but it is as little regarded as that of the sheep led to the slaughter. His God-given intellect obscured in its early morning, is darkened more and more, until it sets in the blackest night of ignorance. Little avails it to him, that poets have sung immortal themes, that philosophers have toiled to reveal the laws of the wondrous universe, that great men have led noble lives or achieved heroic deeds. Of a world beyond the senses he will scarcely ever obtain the remotest glimpse. The Huberts of the factory and mine, more cruel than the Hubert of Shakspeare, have put out the eyes of his mind. They have cancelled the highest and best part of his being.

Do the parents gain by the process? If it be a gain to the working man, for the sake of a few shillings weekly now, to introduce into the labour market a kind of labour which necessarily depreciates the value of his own,—if it be a gain to forego the parental duties of maintenance of offspring, and lose thereby all their filial dependence and attachment,—if to substitute the cold relation of landlord and lodger, for the tender one of parent and child,—if to find the greediness that grasped the children's wages retaliated by the selfishness that consigns the parents' old age and helplessness to the workhouse ;—if this be gain, then indeed the parent *does* gain by sacrificing his child : otherwise it is loss, and loss how great !

It is not even gain to the employer. The intelligence, order, and good conduct of those who serve

him are as important as their bone and muscle,
viewed merely as an element of pecuniary profit.
Many large employers have stated that, even with
respect to young persons, the advantages of the
school discipline have more than defrayed the whole
cost of the schooling. Still greater is the gain to
the employer when the operatives are adults, and
the sum paid in wages forms the largest element in
determining the amount of his profits. What may
he not suffer from their intemperance, their
irregularity of attendance at work, and their want
of economy and care in the use of materials! How
much may he lose by a strike which a few minutes'
conversation with intelligent workmen would have
settled amicably, but which, with ignorant workmen, exasperated by a few leaders equally ignorant,
may end in serious loss, perhaps ruin, to himself,
and desolation to a whole neighbourhood! Certainly, no one's pecuniary interest and personal
comfort are more compromised by popular ignorance
than the employer's; but were he not in the least
affected, or were all the gain from juvenile labour
his own, and all the loss the nation's,—there would
be ample justification for prohibiting so suicidal a
process.

Looking at these difficulties, it appears that the provision of schools and teachers is but a part, and the least part, of the problem of primary education. The much more difficult questions are, how to keep children longer at school? and, nextly, how to supplement the defects of the Day School instruction by other methods? With reference to the first point, much might be done by greater extension of the half-time factory system, under which no child below the age of thirteen is permitted to work above half-time, the remainder being spent in school. The present number of "half-timers" in the borough of Leeds is very small.* No doubt this system, so far as it has extended, has been highly beneficial. In many instances employers have had their attention turned to the question of education, and have had their sympathies and interests awakened in behalf of the employed, not merely in connexion with schools, but in other ways. Parents, whose poverty made even the small earnings of their

		BOYS.	GIRLS.	TOTAL.
* Factory Scholars.	Leeds Township, 1839, . .	230	130	360
	„ Borough, 1851, . .	574	389	963
	„ „ 1860, . .	604	660	1,264

These 1,264 half-timers were employed in fifty-three mills, works, and other establishments.

children an object of importance, have still retained
part of those earnings, and those who care nothing
for the education of their offspring have thus been
very properly compelled to take some share in
providing for it. As respects the instruction acquired by half-time children, it is not, as a rule,
equal to that of whole-day scholars, but the difference is not so much against the half-time system
as might have been expected. Indeed Mr. Red-
grave, the factory inspector, states, "that in schools
under efficient and trained masters, and over
which the managers personally interest themselves,
especially in a Factory School, the 'half-timers' make
as much progress as any scholars in the school."*
The factory half-time system existing before the
present valuable machinery of inspection and grants
was in operation, some Factory Schools, to which it
has not been applied, have, consequently, not par-
ticipated in the improvements which have thereby
been introduced into the ordinary schools. Where,
however, moderate efficiency can be secured in the
schools, it is not an uncompensated disadvantage to
those who must earn their future livelihood by

---

* *Report* for 1860, page 29.

manual labour, that they should thus early acquire habits of industry, and become initiated in the processes which they will have to perform.

The objection to the half-time system is, that it is only applicable (except under countervailing disadvantages) to works where a large amount of juvenile labour is required. Mr. R. Baker shows (and his opinion is confirmed by others) that the half-time system is inapplicable to coal mines. In such cases as mines, agricultural operations, and in all those branches of industry where the Factory School system is inexpedient, Mr. Baker suggests the advisability of a preliminary certificate of education as a condition of employment. In concert with a committee of national schoolmasters, in Bradford, he suggests a certificate of qualifications of the first, second, and third class; those leaving school with only a second or third class certificate, to be required to carry forward their education at an Evening School, until a first class certificate be obtained.*
From Mr. Baker's report† the following remarks upon his plan are extracted, because it appears to be the most practical one yet suggested, and that it

---

* See *Appendix* A.
† *Factory Inspectors' Report*, 1858, page 68.

would meet the great difficulty presented by the contesting claims of juvenile labour on the one hand, and of education on the other.* "The third class qualification is not too high for the humblest capacity, the first not too low for a child of thirteen years old to have attained. * * * I have long been led to believe that either a school certificate ought to be required of a worker, on the first introduction to employment of any kind, or, that instruction should be a condition of the continuance of such employment; that all infant congregated labour should be half-time; that a certain standard of acquirements, to precede educational institutes and associations, should be fixed; after which, compulsion should cease, even though the scholar was under sixteen years of age; but, that in every kind of labour, whether outdoor or diffused, or indoor or congregated, this standard should be requisite at sixteen years of age, if not obtained before then, and should be acquired at Evening Schools, between the months of October and April, as supplementary to the education obtained

---

* Mr. Baker's experience, and his exertions in Leeds and the West-Riding generally, to promote the education and social improvement of the working classes, entitle his opinion to great respect.

before eight years of age, or between eight and thirteen years of age, when at work. The object, of course, of such a plan is, to have every child in school before eight years of age, and to obtain the standard as soon as possible, and with the least interference with labour."

A bill was introduced into the House of Commons,* to prevent any child under twelve years of age being employed in any mine, colliery, factory, workshop, or farm, unless either such child were able to read and write, or that the employer gave an undertaking that the child shall attend school at least twenty hours per month. This measure was defective in two or three points. The penalty was inflicted only upon the employer,—it should also fall upon the parent. The definitions of qualification, viz.,—to read "tolerably" and write "legibly," were rather vague; and surely some arithmetic (say as far as proportion) ought to have been included.

There is this advantage about an educational test: it reaches not only that class of parents who are too ready to sacrifice the education of their children for

---

* April 26th, 1860, by Mr. Adderley and Sir Stafford Northcote. This measure was unfortunately lost, but, it is to be hoped, will be adopted ere long. The principle of it is already sanctioned in factories and mines, and is equally necessary in all other departments of industry.

the sake of their wages, but that class also who entirely neglect to send their children to school, even when there is no such temptation. The Census returns exhibited upwards of two millions of children out of five millions, between the ages of three and fifteen, *neither at work nor at school;* and, though this proportion may have been somewhat reduced, there is still a large number of children whose chances of receiving instruction would be much increased if some such educational test (up to the age of sixteen) were made the condition of employment. How much it might be expected to quicken the apprehensions of ignorant, selfish, or indifferent parents, is illustrated by the following fact, stated by Mr. Baker :—Having had occasion to request certain certifying surgeons to test the educational powers of the children and young persons of between eight and sixteen years of age, who presented themselves for examination for surgical certificates, and a supposition getting abroad that shortly no child would be allowed to work in the mills that could not read,—from that moment the applicants for admission to the schools was so great in the district, that within a fortnight all its schools were filled.*

---

* *Report*, 1859, page 58.

The system proposed has also the great advantage of testing results, and of thus stimulating and improving both Day and Evening School instruction, without interfering with the machinery of teaching itself. A school that did not produce in pupils the desired qualifications, would stand self-condemned, and must either improve or cease to exist. *

---

* " In the highly educated Swiss Cantons, the law which stipulates for education till the age of fifteen, is qualified by a permission to any labourer's child to leave school earlier, on proving his capacity to read and write."—*Speech of the Right Hon. C. B. Adderley, M.P., at the Social Science Association at Bradford.*

CHAPTER III.

SUNDAY SCHOOLS.

AMONG the special characteristics of our country, Sunday Schools form one of its noblest distinctions. No institutions have so united class with class, and to them the superior portion of the labouring classes, whether in the busy manufacturing towns or the quiet rural village, owe much of their knowledge, and the best of their associations. Such a topic demands an Essay by itself; but only one or two salient points can here be alluded to.

The visit of the Queen to Leeds, in September, 1858,—on which occasion all the Sunday School children in the borough were assembled to welcome her,—enables us to present a very complete table of their total number, including all denominations. The following is the summary of Sunday scholars and teachers in the various schools within the borough of Leeds, as returned to the Committee of the Sunday School Demonstration :—

No.	SCHOOLS. Name.	SCHOLARS. Above 8. Boys.	Girls.	Under 8. Boys.	Girls.	Total.	TEACHERS. Males.	Females	Total.	Total.
41	Church of England	4,680	4,753	1,515	1,645	12,593	648	664		1,312
23	Wesleyan Methodist	2,211	2,456	644	700	6,011	660	623		1,283
15	Methodist Free Church	1,288	1,485	447	498	3,718	358	277		635
12	Independent	1,224	1,294	342	337	3,197	263	233		496
10	Primitive Methodist	715	713	285	283	1,996	250	137		387
7	Methodist New Connexion	737	705	205	212	1,859	188	147		335
11	Baptist	717	758	128	152	1,755	158	134		292
3	Roman Catholic	409	471	128	137	1,145	36	46		82
4	Wesleyan Reformers	422	364	90	89	965	123	100		223
2	Unitarian	228	170	31	30	459	43	34		77
5	Neutral, and others	510	499	145	151	1,305	124	28		152
138	Total	13,141	13,668	3,960	4,234	35,003	2,851	2,423		5,274

Evidently a machinery of such extent must form a very important item in the educational provision for the working classes.

One great advantage of the Sunday School system is, that it brings the children under good, or at least harmless, influences, at a time when they might otherwise fall under bad ones. The possession of leisure, the too often unfavourable condition of their homes, and the profligacy of the streets in which they would most probably pass their time, would, save for the Sunday School, have a far more extensively demoralising effect than they now unfortunately have. Often, indeed, besides the gain to the child itself, the religious and moral lessons of the Sunday School have been carried by the child to its home, where parental or family wickedness has felt itself rebuked. Glimpses, at least, of the grand truths of religion, of immortality, the meaning of life and of death, the sense of responsibility, of reverence, come through the Sunday School, and interrupt what, in the case of thousands of children in large towns, would otherwise be an unbroken course of sensualism and virtual atheism.

One very advantageous part of the Sunday School system, is their libraries. In connection with the forty-five (town) schools comprised in the Leeds Sunday School Union, containing a total of 1,576 teachers and 10,832 scholars,* the volumes in their libraries amounted to 20,191. There is reason to believe that the library provision in the Church Sunday Schools, not included in the above return, is in equal proportion. The circulation of these books among the children, and in their homes, is, in itself, a great good.

Although the character of Day School instruction has been so much ameliorated, it has not diminished the extent of Sunday School instruction. On the contrary, as parents have increased in intelligence, they have attached more importance to it,—at least, as keeping their children out of harm's way on the Sunday, if for no other reason.

The total number of Sunday Scholars in 1839, in the township of Leeds, was 11,429, or 13.9 per cent. of the then population. The total number in

---

* *Leeds Sunday School Union (Town Schools).*

YEAR.	SCHOOLS.	TEACHERS.	BOYS.	GIRLS.	TOTAL.
1839	23	799	2,094	2,042	4,136
1859	45	1,576	5,184	5,648	10,832

This " Union" does not include Church, Wesleyan Methodist (Conference), Roman Catholics, and Unitarian Sunday Schools, but generally the Sunday Schools of all other denominations.

1851, was 28,761, or 16.7 per cent; and in 1858, 35,003, or 18.2 per cent. of the whole population of the borough.

One consequence of the improved Day School instruction, as affecting Sunday Schools, has been to lessen the amount of secular instruction given in the latter, and to render them the vehicle of more exclusively moral and religious teaching; and this is their proper function—to *aid* and *complete* the teaching of the Day School, not to serve as a *substitute* for it. Formerly, the largest proportion of children derived almost all the instruction they ever received, from the Sunday School. It was, of course, of a very elementary kind, merely reading and writing, and these often learned very imperfectly. There was then quite enough occupation for the Sunday School, without sending the children to church or chapel to fill up the time.

With the growth of Day Schools, the instruction at Sunday Schools has become more exclusively *dogmatic* in its character,* and the children have

---

* Out of the 10,832 scholars of the Leeds Sunday School Union, 1,617 (768 males and 849 females) are returned as learning writing, and most of this in Evening Schools. No writing is taught in Church, or Wesleyan Methodist (Conference), Sunday Schools.

been required to attend more frequently the various places of worship to which the Sunday Schools are attached. Both these changes are injurious. The first condition of infusing into the minds of youth either moral or religious truth (whatever may be included under those terms), is to *interest* them. Mere dogmatic teaching will not do this, and still less will attendance on public worship, the forms and methods of which are adapted for adults only. On such occasions the children become listless or drowsy, often mischievous, especially when not restrained by a watchful teacher,—but for any intellectual, moral, or spiritual impressions they have derived from the religious services, they might as well have been elsewhere. Of course these remarks apply to young children. Whenever a Sunday School includes in its numbers those who, from age or superior education, are capable of appreciating a more intellectual service, these remarks do not apply.

The difficulty of rendering Sunday School teaching effective has been increased by another cause, viz. :—the separation between the middle and the labouring classes, caused by the removal of the habitations of the former to the suburbs of the

town. Formerly it was the rule, where now it is
the exception, for the middle classes to take an
active part in the work of Sunday School tuition.
As a striking illustration of this, a Sunday School
superintendent states, that whereas twenty years
ago he had a list of forty persons of the middle
classes, as candidates for Sunday School teachers,
for whom there was no vacancy, he has now the
greatest trouble to get one. This duty now mainly
devolves upon the more moral and intelligent portion of the same class to which the pupils themselves
belong,—*i. e.*, the labouring class. The last Report
of the Leeds Sunday School Union even states it as
a matter of congratulation, that "in many schools
half, and in some instances more than two-thirds,
of those who are at present engaged in teaching,
formerly sat upon the benches of those schools."
The motives of the latter are doubtless as pure, and
the sacrifice involved in their self-imposed task is far
greater, than it is in the case of the middle classes ;
but speaking generally, the results are not so satisfactory. A more educated person will always (other
things being the same) possess more influence than a
less educated one. In the action of mind upon
mind, of the teacher upon the taught, sensibility

and sympathy are forces of the highest importance ; and these are qualities far more likely to be possessed by those whom fortune and circumstances have dealt with gently, than by those, however meritorious in other respects, whose life is passed in a hard conflict for almost the means of subsistence. Nor should the influence which mere superior social rank exercises upon those brought under its influence, be left out of account. A working man naturally feels gratified that his children should be taught by his employer, or one of the same rank in life as his employer. Then, too, it is of high importance that what is taught should not be disfigured by the false, not to say grotesque, conceptions, in which well-meaning but unconscious ignorance presents the idols of its own mind as truth. If ever Sunday Schools are to exercise the influence they ought to have, one of the first steps must be to induce persons of superior education to take a personal and active part in them. Next, compulsory attendance at the church or chapel, especially for young children, which only produces a lasting dislike for such places, must be dispensed with. And lastly, the instruction communicated must be less of a mere dry dogmatic character, and more of the teaching that will awaken the intelligence and purify the heart.

If this were done, we should not have to deplore the small results of Sunday School teaching, or that so large a proportion of those whose after career has proved immoral, and even criminal, were so notwithstanding they were once pupils, and even teachers, of the Sunday School.

CHAPTER IV.

EVENING SCHOOLS.

THE deficiencies of Day School instruction have
naturally induced many of the best friends of
popular education to consider what supplementary
methods might be made available. If it were
practicable, it would be delightful to know that the
children of the working classes could be retained at
school long enough to make their education useful to
them. That it is not so, may, in no inconsiderable
degree, be ascribed to the ignorance, and consequent
indifference, of parents,—ignorance thus generating
ignorance, as like produces like. But, in a still
greater degree, it is due to the necessities of the
parents. The first consideration with the mass of
the people, must be the provision of the means of subsistence. Modern civilization has caused their wants
to be numerous, and has at the same time raised
the value of juvenile, as compared with adult, labour.
Against such resistless influences it avails little for
the Educationist to declaim. It is much wiser to

accept the facts, and adapt his methods to them, trusting that, with improved education, its value will be more and more appreciated, and greater sacrifices be made to secure it. The problem is very succinctly stated by the Rev. F. Watkins, Inspector of Schools:—"Given, that children of the working classes leave elementary schools at ten years old, how can they be most intelligently taught and morally trained in other places of education? What can be done by Evening Schools, under whatever name they may be presented to our notice?" Even had the Day School accomplished its proper work,—if, in quantity, quality, and duration, the instruction were far better than it is likely to be for many years to come,—a system of instruction for youths and adults would still be required to render it of much practical utility. It is a common, yet gross fallacy, to suppose that the instruction of a Day School can complete even the merely intellectual training of the humble workman. If the Day School give him mastery of the instruments of knowledge, he yet requires further instruction to enable him to understand the principles of the art by which he lives, and to fit him for social duties and enjoyment. As a very high authority

(Horace Mann) observes :—" More than half the time and labour spent on primary instruction in the elementary Day School, will be spent in vain, unless the educational process there commenced shall be continued afterwards." Of course, the argument for Evening instruction is all the stronger, if it have not merely to complete the instruction of the Day School, but to do its neglected work.

The statistics of Evening instruction in Leeds, were ascertained, in 1858, to be as follow :—

DESCRIPTION.	No. of Schools and Institutes.	EVENING PUPILS.		
		Male.	Female.	Total.
Church of England . . .	16	496	574	1,070
Wesleyan Methodists . .	14	269	308	577
Other religious Denomina-tions	13	488	158	646
*Mechanics' and similar In-stitutes	17	1,289	...	1,289
Total . . .	60	2,542	1,040	3,582

This instruction is given principally during the winter months, almost all teaching being suspended

---

* The statistics of these Institutes are brought down to the present year.

during the summer, from the impossibility of securing the attendance of the pupils. As the population of the borough in 1858 was 191,693, this shows about two per cent. of the population to be under Evening instruction.

Nearly all the Evening instruction is *elementary*. In the 60 schools and institutions giving Evening instruction to 3,582 pupils, 3,331 received elementary, and only 251 more advanced instruction. Though the educational returns of the Census in 1851 were very imperfect in regard to Evening instruction, they strikingly corroborate this statement as to the very elementary character of that instruction generally.*

A further criterion of the quality of the education given in the Evening Schools, is afforded by the pupils' payments.†

---

* In the return of 1,545 adult Evening Schools, reading was taught in 1,305; writing in 1,410; arithmetic in 1,297; English grammar in 339; geography in 344; whilst chemistry was taught only in four schools, and geometry but in two. Recent returns from a large number of Mechanics' Institutes, place four-fifths of their pupils in the elementary classes.

† Analysis of the fees paid by 20,670 members of 105 Institutes in the Yorkshire Union :—

468 pay an average subscription not exceeding 1d. per week.

12,393	,,	,,	,,	,,	2d. ,,
5,397	,,	,,	,,	,,	3d. ,,
2,393	,,	,,	,,	,,	3½d. ,,
19	,,	,,	,,	exceeding	3½d. ,,

Out of the 3,582 Evening pupils,—

1,885 pupils paid nothing.

1,148   ,,   1d. per week.

400   ,,   2d.   ,,

149   ,,   3d. and upwards.

Obviously such fees would in no degree represent the *cost* of instruction even of the lowest kind, if its appliances, such as teachers, rent, fires, &c., were to be paid for. In ordinary Evening Schools rent is rarely charged, the buildings being generally used as Day and Sunday Schools. In most Mechanics' Institutes the rent is merely nominal. The extent to which Evening instruction is dependent upon gratuitous teaching, is remarkable. Out of the sixty Institutes and Schools in Leeds, only five had paid teachers at all, and only one relied principally upon paid teachers. The persons who give this instruction are sometimes individuals moving in a rank of life very superior to that of their pupils : but, in a majority of instances, they consist of shopkeepers, clerks, and the better-educated workmen themselves. They seldom know anything of teaching as an *art*, and possess no other qualification for their self-imposed task, than a somewhat superior degree of information to their pupils, and a generous

desire to raise them in the scale of humanity;—a
sympathy, however, which often makes them succeed
as well as teachers better qualified intellectually, but
who have no enthusiasm in their work. Unfortunately this class is limited, and therefore quite
inadequate to the exigencies of the case. Hence,
if any great extension is to take place in Evening
instruction, it must come through the agency of paid
teachers. But, how are funds for this purpose to be
obtained? If the fees obtainable from the pupils are
added to the few subscriptions likely to be obtained
from the friends of education, they will not suffice
for this large work. But there exists no good reason
why the limited assistance proffered by Government
to Night Schools, should not be made available as
far as possible. By a "Minute of the Committee of
Council on Education" (1st March, 1855), provision was made for giving aid to Night Schools, in
connexion with schools under Inspection. By an
additional "Minute," the Lords of Committee on
Education resolved, on the 26th July, 1858, "to
grant a stipend of £25 per annum to male, and £20
to female teachers, during the probationary period
of two years, following the date at which they
have passed the examination now required for

a certificate, on condition that such period be passed
as second master under a certificated or registered
head master, in a school with an annual average
attendance of not less than seventy-five ; *that
Night scholars may be reckoned with Day scholars
in making up seventy-five ;* "—and, further, "to
allow, where a Night School is organized conform-
ably to the 'Minutes' of March, 1855, the number
of scholars who have attended it on fifty nights
per annum, to be added to the number of Day
scholars, for whom the school may receive Capitation Grants ; * no scholar being reckoned as
belonging to both schools, nor any scholar under
twelve years of age as belonging to the Night
School."

Extracts from the instructions to Her Majesty's
Inspectors of Schools, 24th November, 1858 :—"It
is hoped that the admission of Night Schools to the
Capitation Grants, may facilitate the establishment
of such schools. There are few schools in which the
addition of all local sources of income to the Capitation Grant, will not provide £25 or £30 towards a

---

* Four shillings per pupil, or £15 on seventy-five pupils, attending fifty
nights per annum,—say three nights per week for four months, or two
per week for six months in the year.

teacher's stipend; and this sum, when added to the Government allowance, makes a total which, in the increasing number of certificated teachers, is not below the salary which candidates for employment are likely to be willing to accept in first engagements. The Capitation Grant will provide the means of engaging a second certificated teacher (generally, it may be presumed, a probationer), who may assist in the morning school; singly take the afternoon school, and, if not employed in the special instruction of pupil teachers, assist in the Night School, which the principal teacher will be able himself to conduct. Thus, *two* certificated teachers may be obtained for a Night School, which would be a very great improvement upon the present machinery for Evening School teaching, and would enable Night Schools to be much more extensively established." There is little hope, however, of such aid being made generally available, until the consciences of parents and employers are quickened by the adoption of the principle of a compulsory test of qualification, before children are permitted to work. No amount of pulpit and platform exhortation, no prize schemes, nor any of the many plans for stimulating more attention to education, however good in themselves these aids may be, will be so effective as Mr. Adderley's bill, already referred to, would be, if adopted and faithfully carried out,—that it henceforth be a crime, punishable upon parents and employers, to permit children ignorant of the instruments of knowledge,— reading, writing, and arithmetic,—to work. We should then soon cease to suffer the national disgrace of having nearly two millions of children, of the school age, neither at work nor at school.

It is a serious defect in the "Minutes" granting aid to the Night Schools, that its operation is limited to Evening Schools in connection with Inspected Day Schools. As Sir James Kay Shuttleworth remarks: "Where such a common Evening School already exists as a Mechanics', Literary, or other Institution, its claim for aid is entitled to prior consideration before any rival Evening School be established by the aid of the Parliamentary Grants."*

Whilst it is most desirable that paid and trained teachers should be secured for the ordinary evening classes, there is ample scope and encouragement for

---

* *Second Report of East Lancashire Union of Institutions*, having Evening Schools, page 15.

the assistance of those whose education, opportunities, and inclination, lead them to assist in this
work. As one noble example of what may be done
by the exertions of a few benevolent persons of the
middle classes, we may refer to the Leeds Spitalfields
Sewing School. Its example has led to the formation of two or three similar schools, though none
has achieved an equal degree of success. The
school has an average attendance of from 100 and
200 young women nightly, the number on the books
being upwards of 300, principally girls employed in
the factories, or the daughters and sisters of factory
operatives. The object of its benevolent conductors
is to make the girls better fitted to fulfil their
social duties as wives and mothers. Their method
is stated to be " to teach the girls how, with the
greatest economy to themselves, to buy materials,
cut them out for garments, sew them together, and
mend them when necessary; and also to endeavour
to raise the moral and religious tone of the scholars,
by reading to them, by advice, by encouraging easy
intercourse with them; and by the free expression of
their opinions to their teachers, to obtain the opportunity of easily and quietly, not only checking
what is actually wrong, but showing them what

better educated people would do or say under similar circumstances. We banish," say they, "what may be called all the formal restraints of a school, and mix easily and freely with them in conversation, sympathise with them in their stories of their families and their work, and the joys and griefs of their every day life."

No wonder that such a school should succeed; the wonder would be if it did not. During one year the girls made up 1,300 articles of plain and useful clothing, at a cost to them of £78 13s. No charge is made to the pupils, and the total annual cost of the school, defrayed by a few individuals, is £50.

Such schools show how wide and novel a field exists for the benevolent activity of those who have leisure and education among the middle classes. The demand for female labour has raised its value, and given to women of the working classes a more independent position,—perhaps, however, a doubtful advantage, since it unfits them, to a certain extent, for wives and mothers. Nor have the women of the labouring classes shared to anything like the same degree in the improvement which has taken place in the education of the other sex. Generally they have no intellectual tastes, or none beyond what are supplied by the penny "London Journal" or the "Family Herald." For want of better training, numbers of girls frequent low places of amusement along with youths of the same age. Others starve themselves, or live on tea, coffee, or other innutritious diet, that they may dress in extravagant finery on Sundays. Domestic service, which was once the principal field for female labour, and the best preparation for the future home, is now too much regarded as semi-slavery. Such institutions as the Female Sewing School, if they do not cure, at least mitigate this evil very much. The ability to make the garments of herself and children, the taste for pursuits of an intellectual even though humble character, the refinement introduced by the intercourse with persons of a superior social rank, are all influences of high importance to the welfare and happiness of her husband and children. The secret of the success of this school lies in the fact, that the persons who conduct it are not only superior in social position and education to the taught, but are impelled by the most disinterested and sympathetic motives. Were any considerable number of the middle class to "go and do likewise," a social revolution of the most beneficent character would take place before many years were over. Personal intercourse and sympathy are infinitely better than mere money subscriptions. Quite sure we are that no money subscription can purchase such service ; but those who cannot render it should at least give ungrudgingly, so that the best possible paid teachers might be secured in numbers adequate to the urgencies of the case.

CHAPTER V.

SECONDARY INSTRUCTION.

Sect. A.—THE MECHANICS' INSTITUTE.

THE preceding statements, showing the low state of Evening instruction, even in the merest elements of knowledge, will prepare us to expect a still worse state of matters in regard to the more advanced and scientific instruction of the working classes. While primary instruction has been rapidly improving, secondary instruction, for this portion of the community, can hardly be said to exist in this country.

One reason assigned for the comparative failure of attempts to promote adult instruction, through the medium of Mechanics' and similar Institutions, has been, that the prolonged labour and limited leisure of the working classes prevent them from making acquisitions of any importance. While admitting that excessive toil still precludes thousands from the opportunity, as well as deadens the inclinations, for intellectual exertion, yet, with a considerable number of our people, this is not the case ; and the whole tendencies of the age, as embodied in public opinion, in the limitation clauses of Factory Acts, in the regulations of Trade Societies, and in the attempts to promote early closing, are in the direction of securing a fair amount of leisure to the working classes. The work of the day having exercised only the physical powers, it is felt as rest, rather than as additional labour, to exercise the mental faculties. Besides, the pupils have begun to appreciate the practical utility of their studies in the actual business of life,—they are ambitious to enjoy the social importance which every increase of knowledge confers,—and they are not, as children, sent to school by the act of parents and guardians, but are there by their own free will. Nor ought we to despise the acquisitions made in such limited portions of time as can fairly be spared from the share due to labour and to health. If only a fair proportion of the leisure now devoted to sensual indulgences, were well and systematically employed, their acquisitions might really be very considerable.*

---

* For some valuable remarks on this point, by Captain Owen, in his " *Report on Schools of Art,*" see *Appendix* B.

A more valid reason for our backwardness in this important department of education, is, that unlike primary education, it has not here, as on the continent, had the beneficial co-operation of the State. The Government, it is true, has done a little for art-instruction. It has trained teachers, and has given aid towards paying them, provided models, drawings, and, in other ways, usefully promoted it. And considering the very small amount of assistance rendered, a great deal of actual work has been achieved in art-instruction, especially of late years. But scarcely anything has been done for scientific instruction.

The provision of scientific instruction is the *theory* of Mechanics' Institutes, and while their departure from it has been, considering the circumstances of the case, inevitable, it should not be forgotten that this is their original object,—an object which has never been obtained, except imperfectly, and in a very limited degree. Nothing, indeed, can be clearer on this subject than the following statement, which was appended to the "Rules of the Leeds Mechanics' Institute," when established in 1824 :—

"The object of the Mechanics' Institute is to supply, at a cheap rate, to the different classes of the community, the advantages of instruction in the various branches of science which are of practical application to their several trades or occupations. Such instruction cannot fail to prove of important use to every working man, who is employed in any mechanical or chemical operation; and the scientific instruction which will give a more thorough knowledge of their arts, will greatly tend to improve the skill and practice of those classes of men who are essentially conducive to the prosperity of this large manufacturing town."

With these high aims did the Mechanics' Institution of Leeds start in 1824. So rigidly were the original objects adhered to, that even works of fiction and general literature were excluded from the library. But the deficiencies in elementary education were then too great to render any great success practicable; nor was the exclusion of all works of imagination a defensible step in itself. The Mechanics' Institute rather declined. The Literary Society (established in 1834) supplied the "pleasurable mental relaxation" which the Mechanics' Institute had too much neglected.*

---

* In the first year the Literary Society secured 826 members, and in the second year 863. In 1839 the Mechanics' Institute held an exhibition

The Leeds Mechanics' Institution and Literary Society is now one of the largest and most successful in the kingdom. It has been honoured at its annual soirées by the presence of some of the most distinguished men in the country. By its classes, library, lectures, and newsroom, it has, since its first establishment, given birth to, and fostered intellectual tastes in the minds of hundreds, probably thousands of young men in this town. It has formed a centre * for very many small Institutions in the surrounding districts, which have benefited by its example and encouragement. Such an Institution has high claims to public approval : but it must be confessed that it is the lighter and more amusing departments of the Institution which have succeeded best; and that in its most important

---

of Arts and Manufactures, which realized £1,630, and to which the large number of 183,913 visitors were admitted. With this fund, and £410 contributed by the inhabitants, the present Hall of the Institute, at that time a music-saloon, was purchased for £2,250. The repairs and alterations cost £800, and in 1842 the Mechanics' Institute and the Literary Society became united, to the great advantage of both Institutes. For a table, showing the progress of the Leeds Mechanics' Institution during the last twenty years, see *Appendix* C.

* The Yorkshire Union of Mechanics' Institutes has its centre at the Leeds Institute, and has exercised a most important influence in promoting the formation and success of these Institutes throughout Yorkshire.

department,—the *Classes*,—it has not achieved a proportionate degree of success. Newspapers and Magazines have succeeded; and for his threepence a week, the working man can command, besides the advantages of a reading-room well supplied, the use of a large library, can attend the best lectures, and see all the telegraphic despatches as well as the wealthy man can see them in his club. We do not object, nay, we rejoice at this. But not any or all of these can compensate for the absence, or at least the neglect of, the more strictly educational department. There is a natural tendency in most young persons to the amusing rather than the useful, and these Institutions have constantly to guard against the danger of becoming mere places of amusement, to the exclusion of their more important objects.*

The pupils in the Evening Classes are not more numerous now than they were twenty years ago. Bound by the exigencies of their position. the managers, instead of being enabled to take the true view of what *ought* to be taught, and teaching

---

* The proportion of the number of works of fiction to other literature has gradually risen from twenty-five per cent. in 1850, to thirty-eight per cent. in 1858, and to forty-six per cent. in 1859. No doubt such reading is better than no reading at all, and some of it is highly beneficial, but surely the proportion is far too great. See *Appendix* D.

it, have been compelled to consider what would *pay.*
The question then is resolved into, not what are
the educational necessities of our young artizans;
but, what is required to meet their whims or
caprice,—the love of novelty,—of display,—or the
thirst for excitement. It is a discouraging fact, that
in this large town, where dyeing, tanning, and many
other processes, carried on as they are upon a large
scale, require a knowledge of chemistry, there should
be only one small class, of about fifteen students,
devoted to its study. But the anomaly is in part
explained when we find that the leading Mechanics'
Institution in the town has only a dark, damp,
dingy cellar, which it can devote to this purpose.
We might take each of the other leading trades
which enrich the employers, maintain thousands of
men and their families, and point out how they
also would be followed far more profitably, if there
existed an intelligent appreciation of their principles
by those who pursued them.—(See *Appendix.*)

It is now more than a generation since this
necessity of scientific instruction was acknowledged.
What has Leeds done towards supplying it? A
few small classes have been struggling to maintain
a fitful and languid existence, and that is all.

Great good has been accomplished; nay, the success achieved with the means already employed is the strongest argument for far larger operations in the same direction. In the thirty-six years' existence of the Leeds Mechanics' Institute, its classes, feeble in numbers as they have been, have sent forth many young men, whose superior skill in their calling, and whose success in life, have reflected no small credit on the instruction there derived. We know of instances of the kind, and we have heard of others. But neither the assistance of the State, nor that of the employers of labour in Leeds, has ever placed it within the power of this Institution, or of the friends of education generally, to provide what the case fairly required. There has been no want of such help as could be rendered by newspaper advocacy, nor of the warnings, encouragement, and jubilations which usually take place at the annual soirées, when some peer or literary star honours us with his presence; resolution, moved by the Hon. ——, seconded by ——, Esq., F.R.S., &c., supported and carried unanimously :—"That Education is a fine thing, and that everybody ought to promote it." Next a song by a distinguished vocalist. But when the peer and the guests have

departed, when the lights are put out, and everybody has gone home satisfied, things have resumed
their usual footing till the next annual jubilation,
when all is the same, except the names of some of
the performers. Assuredly this will never erect
the machinery of education ; it will never "supply
to the mechanics and artisans of Leeds the means
of acquiring those branches of science which are
applied to the manufactures of the town," any
more than it would build a ship, construct a steam
engine, or plough a field.

It is right to observe, that the provision of the
library, lectures, reading and newsroom, is sufficiently
in request to be defrayed by the ordinary contributions of the subscribers. But scientific instruction,
if good (and otherwise it is nearly useless), is costly,
and neither the limited interest felt therein by the
working classes, nor their means, render it likely
that it can be supplied unaided. Society, however,
and especially manufacturing centres like Leeds,
have so great a stake in its wider diffusion, that
the public are called upon, out of regard merely
to national and commercial interests, to render
adequate assistance. For the establishment of a
School of Practical Science for working men in

Leeds, two things are wanted. First, accommodation; and, second, qualified teachers, and the means of paying them. The Mechanics' Institute ought to be supplied with a building in which, besides the proper provision for its School of Art, its lecture hall, library, newsroom, &c., there should be ample and commodious accommodation for its chemical class and laboratory, and for the other branches of science. Not less important, however, is the provision of competent teachers. The wise step which the Government took some years ago, to train teachers of Art, they unfortunately have since neglected in behalf of Science teachers; and the consequence is that such teachers could hardly be obtained, if even there existed adequate means of paying them. The Department of Science and Art, however, is now prepared to render valuable aid in the examination and payment of teachers,— the supply of apparatus at half cost,—prizes in books and medals for meritorious pupils,—and assistance in other ways. The department will give aid to the instruction of the working classes in the following sciences :—*

---

* For the conditions and advantages of the new "Minute," see *Appendix* E.

1. Practical, plane, and descriptive geometry, with mechanical and machine drawing, and building construction.
2. Mechanical physics.
3. Experimental physics.
4. Chemistry.
5. Geology and minerology.
6. Natural history, including zoology and botany.

All these branches are of great, and some of them of essential, importance to the industrial occupations of this town. Those arguments which have been so reiterated in behalf of a School of Art, apply with still greater force to a School of Science, because the trade and employments of the town involve the principles of science much more than those of art.* If our manufacturers have reason to dread the competition of French designers,—whose designs, though we may not surpass, we can at least copy,—much more should we dread the competition of the workmen educated in the Trade Schools on the continent. It is well known that in France,

---

* The efforts of the Government to promote a knowledge of art, together with the more general cultivation of taste, are rapidly removing the stigma that rested on this country as compared with France, and are even alarming the fears of the latter country for the continuance of its supremacy.

Prussia, Saxony, Bavaria, and Austria, such establishments have been carefully organised, and have been the means of aiding the efficiency of skilled labour to a high degree.* It is the intelligence of the American workman which enables him to avail himself so largely of the most advanced mechanical appliances. We have had the start in the race of manufacturing industry, and we seem contented to rest upon our temporary superiority. It will be well for us, if we awaken from our conceited supineness in time, that we may not find, too late, like the hare in the fable, that the despised tortoise has won the race!

---

* There are twenty-six provincial Trade Schools in Prussia, which are preparatory to the Central Institute of Berlin. The pupil admitted to the provincial schools must not be younger than fourteen, must know his own language well, and be thoroughly conversant with the elements of arithmetic, the mensuration of plane and solid bodies, and be a good free hand drawer.

The course of instruction extends over two years. The best pupils have the privilege of passing into the Central Institution, and cannot be admitted without a good knowledge of the elements of mathematics, physics, chemistry, and drawing. The instructions are made to have a practical bearing upon the wants of productive industry. The Government defrays half the funds requisite for the support of the provincial schools, and the locality the other half. The charge to the pupils varies from thirty shillings to three pounds per year. In the Central Institute the instruction is gratuitous, and poor pupils receive thirty pounds annually from the Government.—*From Report on Industrial Instruction, Berlyn's translation.*

Sect. B.—THE LEEDS SCHOOL OF ART*

was established in 1847. The outfit of the school and the alteration of premises cost about £350, and the Government granted £80 per year towards the master's salary of £150 per year. A moderate amount was given in public subscriptions; but the School of Design in Leeds, like most of the other Schools of Design throughout the country, proved a comparative failure. Although a general and wide-spread conviction existed that we were deficient in art knowledge, as compared with other countries, yet the public mind was hardly prepared to give practical effect to this conviction. But a deeper-seated cause of failure existed in the fact, that the Schools of Design have been very little, if at all, adapted to meet the practical requirements of industry. Even mechanical and geometrical drawing were left, as before, to be taught by the ordinary teachers of Mechanics' Institutions; and no attempt was made to show the practical connexion of ornamental drawing with ornamental art. No designs for any branch of industry were produced at these Schools of Design, although to train designers had

---

* Formerly School of Design.

been one of their ostensible objects. Drawing from copies and from the antique formed the bulk of the practice, until the pupils got wearied and the public ceased to take interest in them. Since 1852 a great change has been made in the operation of such schools. Their title was changed into that of *Schools of Art*, the instruction was made more practical in its character; drawing was introduced both into the public schools in connexion with the Committee of Council, and into the other public and private schools, and the responsibility and management was thrown more upon the local committees of management. These results were accomplished at a considerable diminution of expense. The actual cost of a lesson of an hour to the children in the parochial schools is so small that no coin will represent it, it being only the one-eighth of a penny per pupil. The consequence of these changes has been a very great extension of the operations of the Leeds and all similar schools; but we have still to regret the want of a sufficient application of drawing to those various branches of industry, where it is so essentially requisite.

The following statistics will serve to show the reader both the large extent of the operations of the Leeds School of Art, and also its principal defect:—

CLASSIFICATION OF TRADE OR CALLING.

Clerks	5
Mechanics	4
Spindle Maker	1
Artists	2
Lithographer	1
Cabinet-makers	4
Wood Carver	4
Architects	5
Tanner	1
Stone Carvers	4
House Painters	4
Coach Painter	1
Engineer	1
Bricklayer	1
Photographer	1
Surveyor	1
Joiner	1
Carpenter	1
Schoolboys	20
Schoolmasters	2
Ladies	15
Pupil Teachers	45
Other occupations	9
Total	133

NO. OF STUDENTS.

General Evening Class	73
Pupil Teachers' Class	41
Ladies' Morning Class	15
Gentlemen's Morning Class	4
Total	133

NO. OF STUDENTS.	
School of Art	133
Children in Parochial Schools taught by Masters from School of Art	1,184
Carried forward	1,317

No. of Students.

Brought forward			1,317
Children in Parochial Schools taught under inspection of Master of School of Art . . .			300
Children of Middle Class School (Mechanics' Boys and Girls) who come to School of Art to be taught			220

HOLBECK MECHANICS' INSTITUTION . .	(All Mechanics) .		16
WOODHOUSE Do. .	Bricklayers . .	4	
	Stone Masons .	3	
	Joiner . . .	1	
	Schoolboys . .	2	
		—	10
KIRKSTALL LITERARY SOCIETY . .	Model Maker . .	1	
	Moulder . .	1	
	Pupil Teachers .	5	
	Schoolboys . .	7	
		—	14
Grammar School Boys			60

Total taught in Leeds . . .		1,937
One Private School . . .		12
Total		1,949

KEIGHLEY MECHANICS' INSTITUTION . .	Mechanics and Artizans . . .	20	
	Schoolmasters and Pupil Teachers .	12	
		—	32
SKIPTON . . .	Schoolmasters and Pupil Teachers .		18
		—	50
Carried forward . . .			50

		NO. OF STUDENTS.
Brought forward . . .		50
BRADFORD . . { Parochial Children . 240		
Pupil Teachers . 20		
		260
HUDDERSFIELD . . { Schoolmasters and Pupil Teachers . 50		
Parochial Children . 400		
Huddersfield College 50		
		500
SLAITHWAITE . . { Schoolmasters and Pupil Teachers .		20
ACKWORTH and FLOUNDERS INSTITUTE . .		200
Total		1,030
In Leeds		1,949
Out of Leeds		1,030
Grand Total . . .		2,979

It will be seen from the accompanying analysis, that out of 2,979 persons taught to draw from the School of Art, Leeds, 1,030 are taught at a distance of above ten miles from Leeds,—1,949 in Leeds and its immediate neighbourhood. Of the 1,949 taught in Leeds and neighbourhood, 1,484 are parochial school children, 292 are middle class scholars, 10 professional students, 29 schoolboys in School of Art and Evening classes, 50 pupil teachers, 5 clerks, 2 schoolmasters, 62 artizans, 15 ladies.

Mr. Walter Smith, one of the head masters of the school, remarks:—

"There is little doubt that, except mediately through parochial schools, the School of Art does not influence the class of artizans in the town for whose especial benefit the school was first established, and on account of whom it deserves the support of the inhabitants.

" There are two reasons for this :—

"1. Until lately practical classes have not existed, and only partially exist now.

"2. There is no room for practical classes. The school as it is, is essentially a drawing school, a cultivator of taste, and a means of the indulgence of taste; but it is neither a practical School of Art, nor does it adequately impart art-power among the body of workmen which exists in Leeds."

At the same time there is displayed some tendency among workmen to make use of the classes which would be of use to them. A large proportion of the new students in the school have come for the special classes,—mechanical drawing, modelling, geometry, and painting. It will, however, be at once evident, that the proportion of workmen who make use of the school as a means of arriving at a knowledge of practical use to them, is very insignificant.

This large amount of work is conducted by two head masters, and two assistant masters. In the central school, besides other branches of drawing, modelling for the use of masons, carvers, &c., and drawing from the living model, are also taught; but the school is crippled for want of proper space and accommodation. If art instruction is to prosper in Leeds, a large and commodious building must be erected, the arrangements of which must be expressly adapted to give all classes general art instruction, and to workmen a practical knowledge of the essential art elements in their various trades. There are hundreds of working men, such as masons, builders, joiners, mechanics, carvers, house painters, upholsterers, cabinet-makers, &c., to whom a knowledge of drawing would be most useful. Along with the proper class rooms, there should be combined an art gallery, where students might not only study from the best models, statuary, and pictures, but which might in the evening prove a pleasant resort for the inhabitants of the town, calculated to refine and elevate the perceptions, to diffuse a love of art, and a taste for the beautiful.

Experience would lead us to expect that, if a fitting receptacle were provided, the munificence and public spirit of the community would fill it. Already some pictures have been given to the Corporation, and we know that several other gifts are merely waiting for a suitable place for their reception.

The attempt, whenever made, to urge forward larger measures for the education of the industrial classes, is often met, even by those who profess to take an interest in popular education, by the objection, that the working classes will not avail themselves of the facilities for self-education, even did these exist,—that they will be created when the demand arises for them,—and that therefore it is premature to take much thought for establishing them until they are wanted. We are not prepared to say that even the majority of the working classes are really anxious about their intellectual improvement, but sure we are that a sufficient desire exists to amply reward every effort made in this direction. The lectures to working men at the London Museum of Economic Geology, the classes of the Edinburgh School of Arts, and many similar instances all over the country, show that numbers can be found capable of acquiring something beyond mere read-

ing and writing, and that if the proper article be
provided, the working man will pay, not the whole
cost, perhaps, but a fair proportion of it. To say
that the working classes do not like to study,
and, as a consequence, to propose to change our
Mechanics' Institutes into places of amusement, is,
as has been justly said, like obviating the difficulty
of getting the poor to church by having comic songs
substituted for the hymns, and an "olio of oddities"
for the sermon. Another proposal to create the
necessary stimulus is entitled to more serious attention,—it is, that the nominations to the smaller
offices of the customs, inland revenue, and post-
office, should be open to those who have obtained
a certain rank in local examinations, conducted by
responsible parties. It would be a calamity if our
people, in any great numbers, looked to Government for the means of regular employment, where
hundreds must necessarily be disappointed for one
who might succeed. If, however, this danger could
be avoided, since these places must be filled,* it would

---

* "There are 12,618 offices, worth from £50 to £80 per annum, in the
Excise, Customs, and Post-office, affording from 700 to 800 annual
vacancies. Also 3,840 clerkships, in the Customs, Inland Revenue, and
Post-office, with about 300 vacancies annually, and a further prospect of
promotion to offices from £300 to £600 per annum."—*First Report of
East Lancashire Union of Institutes.*

be far better to make them the reward of deserving and energetic young men, rather than the price of mere political subserviency. The best preventive to any undue hankering after these situations, as Dr. Lyon Playfair justly shows, will be found in encouraging that kind of instruction most intimately connected with industrial production. The employers of labour are those who can most liberally and most legitimately reward the deserving student of the Mechanics' Institute. It is very important to connect, as far as may be, the student's personal interest with his pursuits, that he should feel that a value is attached to his mental work by those best able to understand its utility. And while there would be no objection, under proper safeguards, to add the field of Government employments to the reward of superior ability and industry, it is a direction that requires carefully watching.

We may very briefly sum up the principal conditions which are essential to the successful working both of Evening Schools and the classes of Mechanics' Institutes. The instruction must be made attractive, or it fails altogether. Young children may be compelled to attend schools, however inferior, merely by the wish of their parents;

but those who attend Night Schools must be *drawn* there. Cold, humdrum, unsympathetic teachers, soon drive away the pupils, and are then too apt to lay the blame of failure on the indifference of the working classes to their own instruction. Hence, it is most important,—

1st. *That the teachers be qualified for the task.* However much we may respect the motives of those who give their services, it is a melancholy spectacle to witness ignorance attempting to teach ignorance. Nor is there anything more opposed to permanent success, as the pupil soon finds out that he cannot learn anything, and discontinues the attempt.

2nd. As a rule, subject to few exceptions, *the teachers should be paid.* Even a small payment will often secure the services of a good teacher, who, being employed in the day, is glad of a trifling addition to his income; and payment, however small, secures punctual attendance.

3rd. The payments of the pupils should be weekly. This plan meets the want and circumstances of the working classes better than any other; besides which, a larger sum can thus be obtained in aid of the expenses of tuition than in any other way; though it has a tendency to occasion irregular attendance.

4th. The instruction should be in a suitable building; that is to say,—in a building convenient for the purpose, well lighted, clean, and comfortably warm, and not too remote from the residence of the pupils.

One most essential method of keeping up the efficiency of educational machinery is by means of periodical examinations, and the public award of prizes and certificates. The Inspection of Day Schools is one of the most valuable features of the operations connected with the Committee of Council on Education. Its value would be much enhanced if the best pupils of every school were annually brought together, along with their parents; and the presence of the chief magistrate, and of the friends of education secured, and some recognition, however small, made on the occasion, of the most meritorious pupils. Nothing would tend more to make both children and parents value education, than to see that it has a value in the eyes of the influential classes. The School of Art pupils, both in the Central and all other schools, are annually examined by the Art Inspector. A Board of Examiners, in connexion with the Society of Arts, for the pupils of Mechanics' Institutes of

Leeds and its neighbourhood, has recently been appointed, the particulars of which will be found in the *Appendix.** This Local Board has only to conduct the preliminary examinations of the candidates; the final examinations being by papers sent down by the Society of Arts, and the Local Committee are expected to make the necessary arrangements for seeing the papers filled up honestly, and according to the prescribed conditions. The experiment is yet new; but, efficiently worked, it may render important services to education. At present the Leeds Local Board of Examiners takes up only the more advanced subjects of study, and pupils under sixteen are not eligible for examination. Now as the Day School for children of the working classes finishes, on the average, when the pupils are ten years old, it would be very desirable to have an examination in elementary subjects for youths between the ages of ten and sixteen, who are in the Evening classes. It has already been shown how desirable it is that Evening instruction should carry

---

* An attempt is now being made to form a Leeds Educational Board, to conduct the Oxford University Examinations for Middle Class Schools, and combining both the Society of Arts Examinations and the Evening Schools Examinations referred to.—See *Appendix* F.

on the elementary instruction which was commenced in the Day School. It is *as* important to afford whatever stimulus can be given by prizes and certificates for good reading, writing, and arithmetic, as for any of the more advanced subjects. If, indeed, we were to judge by the large number of candidates for the Civil Service and other departments, who are plucked from sheer inability to spell ordinary words, it might be said it was more necessary.* An examination of Evening pupils in elementary subjects would tend, if it became effective and popular, to greatly improve the character of the Evening Schools, which, generally speaking, are conducted on no proper system, while the instruction is of the most meagre character. But the most cogent reason of any, is the importance of encouraging children, immediately on ceasing to be Day scholars, to at once become Evening pupils. The age between ten and sixteen is one of the most critical in life, especially for those who, by becoming workers, acquire usually at that period a dangerous degree of independence, and

---

* How defective our system of education, and how needful the examinations for the public services are for the protection of the nation, is shown by the following striking fact from the last report of the Civil Service Commissioners :—Out of 1,972 rejected candidates for the Civil Service, all but 106 failed either in arithmetic or spelling.

far too much freedom from parental control. It would be no great difficulty for the Examiners for Mechanics' Institutes to extend their operations to ordinary Night Schools. Examiners for elementary branches could be found in plenty. A very small subscription would provide prizes and certificates, and the trifling expenses connected with such examinations. Efforts should be made to secure that every boy, as he leaves the Day School, should at once become a pupil of some Night School.

The Philosophical Society would scarcely come within the purview of an Essay on the Education of the labouring classes, but for its Museum, which, with a wise liberality, is open all the year round to the public, at the almost nominal charge of one penny. Its lectures are mainly on either scientific or literary subjects, and during the last five or six years have been of a very high character. They have no doubt contributed in a great degree to encourage and diffuse a taste for intellectual pursuit among the busy, commercial, and manufacturing middle classes, by whom they are principally supported.* The Museum is one of the best provincial Museums in the kingdom. Since the plan of

---

* The present number of members and subscribers is 331.

penny admissions was introduced, the visitors to
the Museum have been as follows :—

YEAR.	VISITORS.
1852—3	1,164
1853—4	8,052
1854—5	7,622
1855—6	7,510
1856—7	7,650
1857—8 *	5,742
1858—9	7,800
1859 – 60	13,500

To make the Museum what it ought to be,—a
place of popular resort,—it ought to be frequently
open in the evening; the only time when the working
classes can attend it. The success which has attended
the opening of the Museum and picture galleries at
Kensington in the evening, is most encouraging.
The Museum itself should be removed to a larger
and more commodious building, as there is no longer
room for the reception of the objects of interest
presented to it. It ought to be, and would be,
something more than a mere lounge for sight-seers,
if competent lecturers were from time to time to
make the specimens of the Museum the subjects of
discourse. To the mass of the community, Museum
means a collection of curiosities, monsters, and *lusus*

* Closed six months, to prepare for British Association.

naturæ. It is true that the Museum is easy enough
of access to the *body* of the working man,—for
scarcely any one is too poor to afford the small fee
of a penny for admission. But as yet there is no
provision whatever for access of the objects to his
mind. Even an explanatory catalogue, or handbook,
giving the leading facts relating to the more remarkable objects, would greatly enhance the utility of
the Museum. The highest value, however, would
be given to it, if, besides the popular lectures just
referred to, it were made the basis of a series of
class lectures, aided by good text books, and followed
by regular examinations in natural history and
geology,—subjects which the Museum is so well
fitted to illustrate.

Sect. C.—Local Educational Institutes.

Besides the Mechanics' Institution and Literary
Society, which ought to be a working man's college,
there are numerous smaller Institutions in different
districts of the town, and which, though they cannot
undertake so high a task, yet form a most important
part of the educational machinery of the working
classes. There are sixteen of these smaller institutes

in the borough.   The following table will indicate
the extent of their operations :—*

For the Year ending April, 1860.	Totals of sixteen local Institutions.	Leeds Mechanics' Institute.	Total.
Members	3,247	1,548	4,795
Annual Income . .	£1,564	£908	£2,472
No. of Vols. in Library	16,494	10,849	27,342
Annual Issues . . .	51,555	45,895	97,450
Periodicals	187	72	259
Newspapers . . .	123	42	165
Lectures	93	28	121
No. of Pupils in Classes	1,140	149†	1,289

It has been doubted by some persons whether
this distribution of many small Institutions is desirable, on the ground that it tends to weaken the
importance and efficiency of the Central Institute.
But if the preceding statistics are correct, not only
are all these small Institutions required, but a very
large addition to the means of Evening instruction
is still wanted, before the state of things in this

* See *Appendix* G.

† These are exclusive of the 133 pupils in the School of Art already given.

respect will be satisfactory. A few years ago a single Institution supplied the intellectual demand of a town even so large as Leeds; nay, it had a struggle for existence,—so limited was the class seeking such assistance. But every successive growth of education increased the numbers of those able and willing to share the pleasures and advantages of the newsroom, the library, and the classes. It then becomes important that such things should have all impediments removed from ready accessibility; be, indeed, brought home to every man's door, just as is the supply of artificial light. It is the tendency of civilization to open up new sources of utility or enjoyment, first to a few, and then to diffuse them in ever and ever widening circles, among the many. It is an advantage, that the feelings and sympathies of the inhabitants of the district are more likely to be enlisted in behalf of these small Institutions, than of the Central Institution, probably some considerable distance from their homes. The district Institutions cannot, of course, yet, nor until education has made much more progress, be expected to provide in the Evening classes anything beyond elementary instruction, in addition to a newsroom and library. The supply of the more advanced instruction ought to be the function of the Leeds Mechanics' Institution. As this Institute already admits the *bonâ fide* members of any other Institute in the town to the chemical class, at the same rate as its own members, the same liberal spirit will no doubt be shown in the other branches of scientific or art instruction.

There is another department of popular instruction that ought to be better organized,—and the merit of the suggestion is due to Dr. Hook;—we refer to the lecture system. Opinions may differ as to the respective merits of instruction by lectures, as compared with other methods; but no one will deny that they are very popular, and highly beneficial. By the present system, however, or rather no system, not a tithe of the advantages of the lectures are enjoyed. The Leeds Mechanics' Institute is the only one in the town which has paid lecturers; and the other claims upon its funds prevent any large and liberal expenditure in this direction. The other Institutes of the town depend upon the gratuitous aid of distinguished strangers, or upon the services (and they are freely given) of our talented townsmen. Now, if an arrangement could be made by which, while each

Institute preserved its own organization, the members of all could enjoy the privilege of attending the same lecture, the following advantages, among others, would obviously result :—

1st. In the case of paid lectures, there might be more of them, and those of the best quality might be obtained.

2nd. Men distinguished by high scientific or literary acquirements, would feel it a greater compliment to lecture to an audience of two or three thousand, or even more, than to two or three hundred.

3rd. Gentlemen of ability, in our own town, would be spared the trouble of repeating their lectures to a number of small audiences in the various Institutions, or the still greater pain of refusing.

4th. The smaller Institutions of the town would then no longer be deprived of lectures, as they frequently are, or be driven to avail themselves of the services of inferior, or, it may be, questionable lecturers, but would then be on a footing with the best Institutions in the country.

Sir C. Lyell tells us that in Boston it is no uncommon thing for two or three thousand people to

attend each of a course of lectures. If our noble
Town Hall is not to be merely a concert-room,
unused nine-tenths of the year for anything but
a show-place for astonishing our country cousins on
their visit to Leeds, to what better purpose could
it be put than the one suggested? Here might
a Whewell, a Hopkins, a Sedgwick, a Layard, an
Oliphant, or a Bowring, not to speak of men of our
own town whom it would be invidious to name,
find a platform worthy of their themes and their
abilities. Here might the Philosophical Society
and the Leeds Mechanics' Institute, the West-End
and the East Ward Mechanics' Institutes, as well
as those of Woodhouse, Headingley, Hunslet,
Holbeck, and others,—the upper, middle, and lower
classes, at one and the same time,—share in the
intellectual feast spread for all comers. Generally,
however, this suggestion would be confined, in
practice, to lectures by men of eminence; or which,
from the nature of the subject or the attractiveness of the illustrations, are likely to excite great
interest; and it must not be supposed that we
would discourage the discourse which may agree-
ably and usefully call together the members of any
individual Institution and their friends, to profit

by the instruction, and in some degree cultivate the good feeling which such meetings promote.

We cannot conclude this general sketch of Secondary Education without remarking, that Great Britain, of all nations, has the deepest interest in its advancement. *We*, at all events, are bound to progress in education, even in spite of the old ladies who trace all the evils that afflict society, as well as their own domestic troubles, to their servants learning reading and writing. Britain has decided for Free Trade and for Free Government, and both of these demand the largest possible development of education. We permit free ingress and egress to the people and commerce of every country in the world, and challenge their competition. We are not now, as we were a generation ago, the sole and undisputed head of the manufacturing and commercial industry of the world. Every nation on the continent is ready to contest the supremacy with us in many branches of production. Iron and coal they have, or can readily obtain; all our mechanical inventions they can purchase from us, or copy; the raw material of wool and cotton they can get as well as we can; and if to all these advantages they superadd, as they have long been doing, workmen well educated in the principles of mechanics, chemistry, and design, we shall soon find that our having had the start in the race of industry and trade will avail us little.

Moreover, we are entrusting the fate of the greatest empire the world ever saw to the hands of the people.   To the people, then, must be given the moderation, the sense of justice, the knowledge of sound political and economical principles, which will make them use that trust rightly.   If free institutions are not to prove a curse rather than a blessing, we must have an intelligent people.   In a word, the problem may be very briefly stated to be—Education or Anarchy ?

Chapter VI.

EDUCATION AND CRIME.

Every philanthropist has his pet theory of crime, and also his remedy. Poverty, intemperance, and ignorance, have each been put forward, perhaps too exclusively, as the cause of crime. Without wishing to underrate the action of other causes, we think that ignorance—culpable, because it is removable—has far more to do with crime than is generally allowed. Be it remembered, that mere ability to read and write is often considered a test of education. If crime is observed to coincide with remarkable uniformity with even these low tests, what influence might we not expect from education, if it were understood in its full import, and universally applied? Against this uniformity, it is no argument to produce exceptional cases of intellectual men whose lives have been stained by crime, any more than that instances of uncleanly or intemperate men who have attained old age is an argument against the influence of cleanliness and temperance in prolonging life. What is it but ignorance which deprives the working man of all power of raising himself in the social scale,—blots out "the hope to rise, the fear to fall," and leaves him an easy prey to every temptation which his own passions, or the vile cupidity of those who batten upon his vices and flourish by his degradation, place in his path? If, by any process, we could secure to every member of the community a superior education, it would go a great way to remove many of those social evils with which it has apparently little or no immediate connexion. It is the ignorant man who unconsciously conspires with his equally ignorant land-lord, to lower the dwelling-house to its meanest standard. It is ignorance of the value of education, which leads the parent to keep his child away from school, and allows it to run wild in the streets; or which forces it prematurely to work, while he riots in drunkenness upon the wages which should be devoted to its intellectual advancement.

The relation of ignorance and crime is shown very specifically by the police and gaol reports. If this relation were accidental, it would not be so general. From the records of the charges at the police-office, we have taken the following totals of five largest classes of offences in Leeds, from October 1st to October 1st, of the years 1858 and 1859:—

		DEGREE OF EDUCATION.				Percentage of well educated persons.
		Well.	Imperfect	None.	Total.	
Drunkenness, and Drunk and Disorderly	1858	52	355	268	675	7.7
	1859	46	345	274	665	6.9
Assaults on Police Officers and Resisting Officers	1858	9	96	79	184	4.8
	1859	9	103	79	191	4.7
Common Assaults	1858	9	91	79	182	4.9
	1859	12	134	126	272	4.4
Neglecting to support Wife and Family	1858	4	43	18	65	6.1
	1859	1	38	21	60	1.6
Malicious and Wilful Damage	1858	2	29	41	72	2.7
	1859	4	27	18	49	8.1

A classification of all such offences as larcenies, acts of vagrancy (prostitution, begging, no ostensible means of living, &c.), breaches of the peace, breaking into shops, highway robbery, burglary, and similar offences, for the two years 1858 and 1859 together, gives the following results :—

Total Offences.	DEGREE OF EDUCATION.		
	Well.	Imperfect.	None.
1,993	26	966	1,001

In 1853 the Town Council published a most valuable return of criminal and miscellaneous statistics of the Leeds Police; since which time, owing to "penny wise" economy, the report has not been published. From this report we find that of 1,702 persons taken into custody for all kinds of offences in 1853, there were—

Of superior education . . . 87
,, imperfect ,, . . . 881
,, without ,, . . . 734

1,702*

These results are confirmed by another authority, in a still more striking form. The valuable Report of the Leeds Borough Gaol for 1859, shows the state of ignorance among the criminal class.

* Out of 118,162 persons summarily convicted in 1858 in England and Wales, 41,826 could neither read nor write, 68,227 could read and write imperfectly, and only 397 are returned as possessed of superior instruction.

Classification of 1,866 prisoners committed during the year:—

Can neither read nor write . .	660
Can read and write imperfectly .	1,171
Can read and write well . . .	33
Of superior education . . .	1
Not ascertained	1
	1,866

A large proportion appear to have attended Day and Sunday Schools; but unless we knew for how long a period, this fact tells us little. The degree of instruction, when more particularly analysed, is as follows:—

	Per cent.
READING.	
Ignorant of the names of the letters	7.28
Acquainted with the alphabet .	18.29
Could read a little . . .	18.22
Could read fairly	19.46
Could read well	36.73
WRITING.	
Unable to write at all . . .	47.81
Could write their own names and no more	23.32
Capable of writing a letter . .	26.53
Good writers	2.33
ARITHMETIC.	
Entirely ignorant . . .	72.08
Could perform the simple rules .	19.82
The compound rules . . .	5.83
The higher rules	2.25

That these people *could* have been taught, is proved by the great improvement made by them in these very branches of knowledge, while in prison for comparatively short periods. How much, or how little, education "might, could, would, or should" have done for them, it will be time enough to enquire, when the large majority of criminals are returned in gaol statistics as "well educated."

It is not intended to attach undue weight to the facts disclosed by these statistics. No doubt the persons returned as of superior education are, from circumstances and social position, free from many of the greatest inducements to crime. The returns show a larger number of offences committed by persons of imperfect education, than those who have had no school education at all. It must not be inferred that the former have a greater propensity to crime; but that, owing to the diffusion of schools, and other means of popular education, the mass of the community have acquired at least a smattering of knowledge, and that hence, being the largest class, it supplies the greater proportion of criminals. After all allowances, the difference shown by superior education in lessening criminality is enormous, and sufficient from this point of view alone to justify the community in any expenditure, and in exertions however great, to secure to every person the means of the best possible instruction. There is also this encouragement, that the criminal class is in itself a very limited one. It is numerous breaches of the law on the part of a few, rather than numerous transgressors, that make up the fearful catalogue of crime.* Stop the primitive rill, and you will lessen or dry up the broad stream that flows from it. Hence, too, though a far greater increase of ordinary instructional machinery, such as schools and educational institutes, is desirable on other

---

* Number of prisoners committed during the year, who have been previously committed to the Leeds or other prisons:—

	Males.	Females.	Total.
Once	239	96	335
Twice	119	47	166
Thrice	72	30	102
Four times	52	16	68
Five times	33	11	44
Seven times and above five .	42	23	65
Ten times and above seven .	17	24	41
Above ten times . . .	5	21	26
Total . .	579	268	847

grounds, it is not so much to these as to other
special agencies which are adapted to meet the case
of the pauper and criminal classes, that we must
look for the most effective action on crime, and
which, indeed, might be distinguished by the title
of "Preventive education."*

---

* "It is now well known that crime in England is, to a very great
extent, hereditary and professional; that it proceeds from a much more
limited and distinct class than used to be imagined; and from this class—
the *homeless* class—our National Schools do not draw. The *home-bred*
classes (if I may so use the word, as the opposite of *homeless*) are indeed
supplying the criminal class with recruits, seduced by the temptations of
drink or poaching; and the number of those who thus lapse into crime
may be, and is confessedly, reduced by the operation of our National
Schools. But for direct aggressive action upon the crime-breeding class,
society must look to other agencies, of a penal or reformatory kind, and
not to the National Schools. The province of the National Day School
is to make the home-bred child more wise and virtuous, rather than to
reclaim the homeless."—*Rev. J. P. Norris. Report of Committee of
Council on Education*, 1859-60, p. 104.

CHAPTER VII.

PAUPER AND CRIMINAL EDUCATION.

THE class of children who constitute the principal source from which the mass of future adult criminals is formed, may be conveniently divided under four heads :—

First. Children deprived of one or both parents, and who require maintenance as well as education. For this class of children it is alike the dictate of humanity and policy to provide an asylum. In this respect Leeds has done its duty nobly. There is no institution in the town of which we may be more justly proud than the Industrial School, under the control of the Board of Guardians. Its erection cost £17,000, and it will accommodate about 400 children. It now contains 221 children, the upper division, consisting of about 60, spend half their time in school, the other half in industrial work —the boys being employed either in gardening, tailoring, or shoemaking, the girls in domestic duties and sewing. The children are fed, clothed, and educated, at a weekly cost of about 6s. 2d. per head. The education is practical and useful, and as soon as the children are of a suitable age, they are drafted off to fill appropriate situations. About 50 children per annum are placed out in life, either as apprentices or domestic servants, and the failures are as low as two per cent. The applications for them are more numerous than can be supplied. A visit to the school is a most gratifying spectacle. Contrast the light airy apartments, the long rows of clean comfortable beds, the alternations of school instruction, work and play, with what, but for the existence of this institution, must have been the fate of these 230 little ones. Such as had not perished, would have been brought up among scenes of vice and misery, and crushed both in body and mind.

The second class of children is that whose parents are beggars, thieves, prostitutes, receivers of stolen goods, and of no calling whatever,—the refuse of the town. Such children are trained up as vagrants, mendicants, and petty thieves; and thus left to themselves, are nearly sure to fall into a career of crime. Considering the great utility of the Industrial School, and that an increase in the

numbers would make no proportionate increase in
the expenses, it seems a pity that its vacant space
is not made available for this class. The Industrial
Schools Act of 1857, gives magistrates power to
commit to these schools, children, who, by mendicancy
or other petty infringement of the law, render
themselves amenable. The Committee of Council
on Education offer the sum of 3s. per week towards
the maintenance of each committed child. The
parent can also be required to pay towards the
support of such children. Why should not the
beneficent provisions of this Act be applied to
Leeds ?* It is, however, inconsistent, that while
the expense of maintaining a child convicted of
vagrancy costs as much as one convicted of theft,
the allowance from the State towards the expense
of each should be so different. Whilst a child is only
very *likely* to become a thief, the State allows 3s. per
week for his maintenance; after he *has become* one, 7s.
Not only is it wiser to catch the criminals a little
younger, and send them to the Industrial School,
but it is unfair to devolve the maintenance of such
pupils upon the Ragged Schools, which have quite

---

* Through the action of the Industrial School in Aberdeen, such an
object as a begging child is a very rare sight.

enough to do in providing Day School instruction
for the outcasts of the streets, without being
burdened with the task of organizing a new provision for their support as inmates.   It seems like
playing at cross-purposes, to institute a new
machinery when a better one already exists, not
made available to half its capability.   The children
whom we would especially endeavour to reach by
means of the Industrial School, are those of whom
it may be said that they had better have lost their
parents, than have them so debased.   They grow up
amid filth, rags, and wretchedness, with no school
but the street, no schoolmaster but the policeman,
no conscience, and no fear save that of detection.
These little outcasts imbibe the language, manners,
and habits of the low neighbourhoods where they
resort.   To swear, lie, steal, and to revel in premature
sensuality, are but the normal and ordinary conditions of their lives.   They look upon society as a
prey, the law as an enemy, the gaol almost as an
asylum.   Surely if ever there were a case where a
little gentle coercion is justifiable, both for the
interests of the child and of society, this is one !

A very salutary provision exists, empowering the
Poor Law Guardians to give education to the

children of persons in receipt of out-door relief.
Under the operation of this Act (18 and 19 Vict.
c. 34, 1855) 229 children are receiving intruction at
various Day Schools. Unfortunately the law is
defective in not rendering such education compulsory.* The consequence is, that though this boon
is offered in all cases, a greater number refuse
than accept it.

The third class of children consists of those whose
character and condition is a little above that of the
children just described. If not too good for an
Industrial School, they have at least not yet committed any illegal act, but cannot be induced to
attend any ordinary Day School, owing to their
ragged and dirty condition. For such children those
excellent institutions, the Ragged Schools, have
been devised. In Leeds there are two such schools
established : one at Richmond-hill, the other in the
Leylands; and both situate in the very centre of
the most neglected districts of the town.†

The children who attend the Ragged Schools are

---

* The 3rd section of the Act is : " Provided also, that it shall not be lawful for the Guardians to impose as a condition of relief, that such education
shall be given to any child of the person requiring relief."

† For a full account of the operations of these schools, see the Report of
the Committee. *Appendix* H.

drawn thither by kindness. They have to be sought out, and probably it is no small inducement to them to attend, that they receive a dinner,—very humble, certainly, but a great improvement upon what they would otherwise get. While some seem pale and stunted, the majority are healthy, and the aid of a warm bath and good clothes would in an hour transform them into as good-looking children as those of any class of the community. They learn the ordinary rudiments of education, appear to be quite amenable to discipline, behave themselves very well, and enjoy their games and plays in the neighbouring street and in a little back playground, as though sin and sorrow, starvation and rags, were entirely unknown. Among the benefits already derived from the school, a shopkeeper stated to the teacher, that shortly after its establishment he ceased to suffer from petty depredations as formerly.* The schools are at present supported by the subscriptions of a very few benevolent men, who cannot, and ought not to be expected, to assume per-

---

* In 1855 a Ragged School was established at Bradford, and the police books that year recorded 111 cases of juvenile delinquency. In 1856 they fell to 76 ; in 1857, to 47 ; and in 1858, to 26.—*Transactions of the Social Science Association.*

manently an expense properly devolving upon the whole community. The subscriptions ought to be spread over a much larger number of contributors, as they might be, if small amounts were taken and collected regularly, for which at present no machinery exists. Such schools ought, in addition, to receive the Parliamentary Grant and regular Inspection,* which would doubtless prove not less advantageous than in the ordinary National Schools.†

The fourth class is that of juvenile offenders who have broken the law, but whose youth justifies the belief that they are still open to the influence of education. Formerly such a youth would have been committed to prison, there to herd with hardened adepts in crime and villainy; and while every latent good impression would have been speedily erased, he would rapidly have graduated in the qualification suited to ensure his repeated committals to the gaol. *Out* of prison he became a depredator

---

* This has been done in some instances, but difficulties are thrown in the way by the Government, which seems not to recognize its proper duties in this direction. See *Paper by Mary Carpenter*, in *Transactions of Social Science Association* for 1859, p. 397.

† For details as to the aid granted by the Committee of Privy Council on Education, see *Appendix* I.

and pest; *in it*, an expensive pensioner to society.
This has now been changed, and the improved tone
of public sentiment regarding education and the
causes and cure of crime, is nowhere better evinced
than in the general establishment of Reformatories.
Here, too, Leeds has not been behind. A Juvenile
Reformatory has been established at Adel, which,
though having no architectural pretensions, is a
thoroughly practical institution, adapted to its
purposes. It contains about 60 inmates, the
majority of whom are boys. Its object, stated in
the rules, is "to promote the reformation of boys
convicted of crime, by training them up in habits of
industry, in out-door and other employment, im-
parting to them an education of a plain character,
and, especially, by an earnest endeavour to bring
them under the influence of religious principles, and
also by placing them out in suitable situations on
their discharge from the Institution." The boys
and young men perform the principal part of the
industrial operations. Some of the boys work as
masons, shoemakers, and joiners; some at smith's
work; others at washing, baking, and other household employment; the rest in agricultural labour.
The cost of each boy, per week, in the Reformatory,

is 7s. 9d.* Government contributes 7s. per week; the West-Riding Magistrates, 2s. 6d. per week for each boy they commit; the Town Council, nothing. The subscriptions amount to £148 18s. 6d. Two-thirds of the boys are from Leeds, and one-third from the West-Riding. It is probable that the Government allowance will be sufficient to meet the wants of the place, when all the extras are completed, and the land is got into cultivation. Four boys were sent to Canada last year, who have done remarkably well, and Colonel Rhodes- has sent for five more for his friends. One of these four was a housebreaker, and had never worked in his life, and another was the head of a class of young thieves in Leeds. In the hours not devoted to manual labour, the inmates are taught various branches of elementary knowledge, and

---

* Thus estimated :—

Cost of food per week	2s. 6d.
Cost of clothing per week . . .	1s. 2d.
Cost of washing, fuel, light, printing, school expenses, and rewards to boys . .	11d.
Probable cost of salaries when they have the full number, 50	2s. 0d.
Outfits for boys leaving, expenses in sending boys to Canada, &c.	1s. 2d.
	7s. 9d.

receive daily religious instruction. Many of them
are so eager for improvement as to devote their
play-hours to study. In the words of the last
Report, the conduct of these poor boys is "good,
—good as compared with that of ordinary boys ;
wonderfully good, when the former lives and
principles of these particular boys are taken into
account." They are treated as members of one
family, firmly yet kindly, with scarcely any surveil-
lance, and are frequently even sent on errands to
Leeds, "*with no guarantee for their return, or their
conduct, beyond their own sense of duty, or their
feeling of attachment to the place.*"*

Such facts help us to the methods of dealing with
criminals and crime. While discarding all maudlin
sympathy with the criminal, we must yet see that
he is of the same nature with ourselves, that had we

---

* The tendency of Reformatories to diminish the amount of Juvenile
crime may be estimated from the following table of Commitments of
Juveniles under sixteen, for 1856, 1857, 1858, and 1859:—

	1856.	1857.	1858.	1859.
Boys . .	11,808	10,822	8,837	7,582
Girls . .	2,173	1,679	1,492	1,331
	13,981	12,501	10,329	8,913

Showing a decrease of nearly 14 per cent. on 1858, of nearly 29 per cent.
on 1857, and above 36 per cent. on 1856.

been treated with the same neglect, or exposed to the temptations, *we* should have been as *he* is; that even as he is, he is still human, and has the feelings and instincts of humanity; that so long as all hope, all aspiration, is not utterly dead within him, so long is there a possibility of making him a good member of society; and above all, that *prevention*, not *punishment*, is the true method of dealing with crime.

Chapter VIII.

SOCIAL EDUCATION.

THERE are some agencies which, though they cannot be classed as schools, have an educational influence of the most powerful kind. That view of education which limits it to mere scholastic instruction, is narrow and incomplete. Let any one analyse the influences that have formed his own character, and he will find he has had many more "schools and schoolmasters" than those which commonly pass under those names. Just so with any community, whether comprising a nation or a town. Whatever tends to render the conditions of social existence more favourable,—physically, intellectually, or morally,—has an *educative tendency.* The character of the ordinary literature of the working classes,— the possession of the means of comfortable support, —habits of economy,—the character of the streets and dwellings,—the kind of amusements,—all exercise a most potent influence in educing or stunting the faculties and moulding the character. Although we have hitherto only dwelt upon that school education which falls more specifically within the scope of this Essay, a few remarks on collateral topics may not be out of place.

Throughout the country a very decided improvement has taken place in the character of the literature perused by the working classes. The improvement, commenced a generation ago by the Society for the Diffusion of Useful Knowledge in their "Penny Magazine," and the "Saturday Magazine" of the Christian Knowledge Society, immediately followed by the publications of Charles Knight and Chambers, has, during the last ten years, gone on at a greatly accelerated ratio. Since that time, the "London Journal" and the "Family Herald" (the periodicals of largest circulation among the operative classes) have greatly improved; and John Cassell's publications have replaced the numerous ones by Lloyd, and are an immense improvement thereon. There used also to be issued several serials of an immoral and profligate character, but they are nearly all extinct. The only ones now published to which the term immoral can be properly applied, are two reprints from stereotypes, which will probably issue as long as the plates last. The penny newspaper press is very good in its character, and its daily circulation is now six times greater than the circulation of all the daily papers before the penny press.

Tolerably complete statistics have recently been obtained by Mr. John Pickering, Secretary of the Leeds Mechanics' Institution, of the circulation of newspapers and periodicals in Leeds; the total results of which are as follow:—

Circulation of Newspapers and Periodicals in Leeds, May, 1860.

	NEWSPAPERS.		PERIODICALS.		TOTAL.
	Daily.	Weekly.	Weekly.	Monthly.	
Literary and Scientific	...	...	19,727	6,454	26,181
Religious . .	...	...	2,375	7,968	10,343
Temperance .	...	...	374	14,672	15,046
Total . .	2,540	24,937	22,476	29,094	51,570

The particular items of which this table is composed will be found in an *Appendix*,* and afford interesting indications of the character of the

---

* See *Appendix* J.

popular literature. Compared with data of the same kind, obtained by the Rev. Mr. Hall in 1852 and 1858,* there seems to be a considerable improvement, both in quantity and quality.

The amount of money expended per annum in the above publications is as follows:—

	Weekly.	Monthly.	Total.
Literary and Scientific	£4,564 3 10	£1,201 0 0	£57,65 3 10
Religious .	485 15 4	833 10 6	1,319 5 10
Temperance .	81 0 8	564 14 6	645 15 2
	Daily.	Weekly.	
Newspapers .	4,021 4 0	11,841 1 0	15,862 5 0
			£23,592 9 10

Mr. Pickering estimates that of this amount there is expended—

By the working class	£9,244 11 10
By the middle and upper classes . .	14,347 18 0
	£23,592 9 10

Leeds, fortunately, suffers less from poverty than most manufacturing towns, owing to its possession of numerous and distinct departments of productive industry, which prevent the serious fluctuations experienced by towns mainly dependent on a single branch of manufacture. Wages are not high, but

---

* See *Report of Yorkshire Union*, 1859, p. 29.

they are more certain. Rents also are low; and the neighbourhood of a well-cultivated agricultural, as well as a rich and well-wrought coal district, together with facilities of conveyance, insure cheapness of both food and fuel. Thus the large majority of the working classes are free from that extreme indigence which is sometimes a fostering cause of despondency, followed by recklessness and crime.

The working classes of Leeds show a very creditable amount of economy, though doubtless there is still much room for improvement. In the Leeds Savings Bank there are 12,411 depositors* (8,144 males, and 4,267 females), and the amount of deposits on the 20th November, 1859, reached the large sum of £339,890 12s. 8d.: allowance must be made for the fact, that a portion of this amount was for Trust accounts and charitable societies, and also that the Bank embraces a district beyond the borough. Besides this Bank, there are in Leeds eighteen branches (comprising about 3,600 depositors) of the West-Riding Penny Savings Bank, with deposits to the amount of £2,000; in addition to many other similar Penny Banks in

---

* For a classification of the *employments* of these depositors see *Appendix* K.

connection with schools and places of worship.*
Several Building Societies must be noted, one of
which (the Leeds Permanent Benefit Building
Society) has received from its members, in the
twelve years it has been established, the sum of
£750,532 9s. 0d.† Add to this the Sick Benefit
Societies, under various names, containing probably
about 36,000 members, insured against sickness, and
for a sum at death. Then there is the Co-operative
Flour and Provision Society, consisting of 3,000
members, possessing a capital of £10,000, employed
in furnishing themselves with flour, groceries, and
other articles, at the cheapest rate. Here is the
germ, which it only requires an increased intelligence and self-denial on the part of the working
classes, to develop into one of the most gigantic

---

* It is most important that these Penny Banks, now so rapidly spreading,
should be well organized, and strict precautions taken to ensure safety, as
any fraud or failure among them would destroy the confidence of the
working classes in them, and do incalculable injury. A proper method
of keeping the accounts, a guarantee for the funds, and a fair per-centage
of interest is ensured to the Penny Banks affiliated with the West-
Riding Penny Bank, of which there are now (July, 1860,) 92 branches,
containing 15,000 depositors and £16,000 in deposits. For the conditions
and advantages of this Bank, see *Appendix* L.

† This large sum was paid by 16,221 members and depositors of loans.
The total amount invested was £382,627 4s. 10d. by 1,280 borrowing
members.

social revolutions. It would be easy to accumulate similar facts, but these will suffice to indicate how *much* the working classes are doing to elevate their social position. In a few large establishments, Sick Clubs and Savings Banks have been established with the best results, and there is no reason why they should not exist in all mills and workshops of any magnitude. The employers should encourage and aid them, if only from a regard to their own interests, but any interference in their management would be injurious, perhaps fatal.*

The physical condition of the majority of the working classes of the town would have been good, had it been subjected to proper municipal regulations during the last thirty years. Decent houses and well-drained streets are scarcely less important than good wages, or Day and Sunday Schools; but notwithstanding an enormous sum expended in making drains, there are many miles of houses, yards, and streets, *unconnected* with the main drainage !

In Leeds the reprehensible mode of building cottages back to back, has been almost universally the custom, and in spite of its known evils, it is allowed to go on, no steps being even contemplated

---

* For illustrations of well-managed clubs of this description, see *Appendix* M.

to check its growth. The unfortunate dwellers in miserable streets so constructed sometimes struggle for a while to maintain an aspect of decency about their little dwellings, but at last the accumulating filth renders it impracticable, and they give up the contest in despair. One privy to *four* cottages has been settled to be the *legitimate* allowance in Leeds ; but this liberality of supply has been by no means universally attained. A favourite plan, and almost inevitable upon the back-to-back system of building, is to plant the privies for a number of houses in the centre of the row, with a sleeping chamber over them ! Every question of convenience, or even of common decency, seems sacrificed to the one consideration of getting the largest possible return for the money invested.*

---

* In this, as in all other investments of capital, the builder of cottages looks merely to the profit in interest of his money; and perhaps the only mode, or at anyrate the likeliest way, of getting better dwellings for working people, would be by the formation of companies, which, by purchasing a site of adequate dimensions, might erect dwellings combining all needful provisions for health, and economy in cooking, washing, and other needful household affairs,—a space of ground for drying clothes and children's recreation; and which there is now experience enough to shew can be done at a fair profit, and with a perfectly safe investment. A few such groups of houses would compel greater attention to these necessary provisions on the part of *all* builders. And if the decent working man would set down a few requisites for his abode, and as far as practicable insist on having them, builders would bid for tenants having such notions, —the best evidence of their being trustworthy tenants.

To add to these evils there is, of course, the gin-shop and the beerhouse, as if to blot out the last lineaments of humanity, already nearly destroyed by the other associations of these wretched neighbourhoods.

" Vices festering to despair,
Or sorrows petrifying to vices ; not
A finger touch of God left whole on them ;
All ruined, lost—the countenance worn out
As the garments, the will dissolute as the act,—
The passions loose and draggling in the dirt
To trip the foot up at the first free step !"

No one can ever tell, statistics cannot reach the vast amount of evil done, and of good arrested, by these places. A distinction must, however, be drawn between some public-houses and a few of the more respectable beerhouses, generally well conducted, and the dramshops and lower class of beerhouses. Apart from the besotting influence of the drink, the low beerhouse is too often the focus of depravity for a whole neighbourhood, a place where gambling and card-playing constitute quite as great attractions as drinking, and where prostitutes are regularly kept. Often they are resorted to by mere youths of both sexes, who speedily lose the good impressions they may have gained in the

Day or Sunday School, and where they rapidly
graduate in vice and criminality. Then there are
other places where the attractions are perhaps less
coarse, but not less seductive, nor ultimately
less pernicious—the casino and singing rooms.
Comic songs of a more than doubtful character,
recitations spiced with *double entendre*, dancing,
semi-dramatic performances, and mere buffoonery,
accompanied by tobacco smoking and drinking,
are the ordinary attractions of such places. One
place of the kind in Leeds has a larger nightly
attendance than the Evening classes of all its 17
Mechanics' Institutes put together!

If, as we believe it may be assumed, that the
proportion of public-houses and beerhouses to population is about the same in the out-townships as
within the township of Leeds, the statistics collected
by Mr. Baker, in 1839, will show that there has been
a very great decrease of this pernicious influence in
the last 20 years, owing doubtless to the progress of
popular enlightenment, and especially to the exertions of the Temperance Society. In 1839 there
was one public-house, or beerhouse, to every 182 of
the population (township), whereas in 1860 there
was only one such house to every 266 (borough), or

a decrease of 31 per cent. in proportion to the population.* Had it not been for the beerhouses, in
which almost the entire increase has taken place, the
improvement would have been greater than it is.†

These evils have been alluded to from the conviction, that before the machinery of education,
however perfected, can produce any great and
striking effect upon the mass of improvidence,
profligacy, and crime, the other conditions of a
correct social life must be inaugurated. Better
cottages and streets, and fewer drinking houses, are
essential.

Another important element of individual and
social education, is the public amusements; and
their character (whether as cause or effect) is no
bad index to that of the people themselves.

The ancients very wisely treated their games as
national institutions, and the Greeks especially made

---

* The following are the statistics referred to in the text :—

	Year.	Inns.	Beer-houses.	Total.	Estimated Population.	Proportion.
Township .	1839	215	235	450	82,121	1 in 184
Borough . .	1860	380	341	721	In 1858, 191,693	1 in 266

	1839.	1860.
† *Inns* in the Township of Leeds . .	215	238

them contributory to both mental and physical development. Among ourselves, the stimulus of private gain is trusted to supply whatever amusements are demanded by the people, whose tastes are, therefore, pandered to instead of elevated, and this with no check except the lax one of public opinion, and, in extreme cases, of police regulation.

Impressed by the evils resulting from the amusements ordinarily presented to the working classes of Leeds, a few gentlemen, in 1853, established a society called the "Rational Recreation Society." Owing to want of means, it never went beyond affording cheap Saturday evening concerts. It once made an unproductive appeal to the public on behalf of a gymnasium. The effect of the society's operations was in a great measure to supersede the system of full-dress expensive concerts, and to present the public with the highest class of music at a very moderate price. This was a great benefit, but unfortunately it reached mainly the middle class, and those in social positions immediately above the operative classes; in this respect strikingly corresponding to Mechanics' Institutions, which, however beneficial, have not sufficiently reached the class to whom they nominally belong. During the seven seasons the concerts were held in the Music Hall, the proportion of the total admissions was as follows :—*

At 3d.	.	.	.	26 per cent.
„ 6d.	.	.	.	41 „
„ 1s.	.	.	.	33 „

and during the two seasons the concerts have been held at the Town Hall, the proportions have been as follows :—

At 3d.	.	.	.	33 per cent.
„ 6d.	.	.	.	33 „
„ 1s.	.	.	.	34 „

Besides the above concerts, 20 evening organ performances were given in 1859, at a charge of 3d., and yet the highest number present was 794, and the average attendance only 544. These facts are not very encouraging, yet there is no doubt that the taste for good and refined music is rapidly diffusing. It has not yet reached the operative classes to any considerable degree, and it may be doubted whether the attendance at the lowest places of entertainment has been appreciably diminished. When there is a circus, however, or any popular spectacular entertainment, the beerhouse keepers are loud in their complaints of the serious diminu-

---

* See *Appendix* N.

tion in their receipts. The drama in Leeds is very inferior, and such as would not be tolerated in the smallest continental town ; and the associations connected with the theatre generally are, it might almost be said, so incurably bad that it is in vain to speculate upon what might be done by it under better arrangements. The attendance at the theatre when a dramatic performance of the higher order, by artists of acknowledged merit, is given, proves that there is no want of appreciation for excellence, in what might be the most elevating of recreations, and the instrument of rendering our people acquainted with the noblest poetry in the world. A new theatre ought to be erected in Leeds, and if the middle and upper classes supported it, it would be commercially remunerative, and thus enable it to dispense with the representation of pieces of an improper character, and to remove the grosser associations connected with it. The attractiveness of this kind of amusement is manifested in the crowded audiences that attend dramatic readings in the Mechanics' Institute, and operas in the Town Hall, stripped of the action and scenery of the drama, and which serve as occasional and successful substitutes.

Leeds has no doubt enough of the ruffianism which culminated recently in the national prize fight ;* but on the whole it is more than usually free from gambling, and those brutal and cruel sports which, in the face of " Bell's Life," are fast dying out in this country. Its amusements are less gross and less demoralizing than in most other large towns. All classes are fond of out-door amusements, to which Woodhouse moor, now the property of the town, and the beautiful scenery in the neighbourhood, give special inducements. Much, however, yet remains to be done to render out-door recreations available to the great majority of our operatives. Woodhouse moor has now been drained, but it ought also to have a good carriage road round it, planted with trees, and interspersed with shrubs and flowers; and horses should no longer be permitted to injure the surface, and make it unfit for walking or games. The moor would then become a resort at all times pleasing to the eye, and especially grateful in hot weather. In one corner a gymnasium might be placed, similar to those in the people's parks at Manchester, which form such an admirable counter-

---

* Many thousand copies of the account of this disgraceful exhibition were printed and sold in Leeds.

active to the evils of confined and sedentary employments.* Woodhouse moor, however, is from its situation incapable of meeting the wants of the industrial thousands in the crowded townships of Hunslet and Holbeck, and at the East end of Leeds, who need far more the invigorating and refreshing opportunities of such exercise grounds than do those of Headingley. Hunslet and Holbeck moors should, also, be secured, and made pleasant and perpetual places of resort for the inhabitants. The growth of manufactures and trade is crowding the people into still narrower spaces, where the fresh breath of heaven is oppressed with noisome gases, and the blue sky dimmed by smoke. The accumulation of wealth is fencing round every green field, and enclosing every moor. The river, that once flowed free for all, and nearly as pure as its source,

---

* The Rifle Corps movement is an important adjunct to the promotion of physical education. If properly conducted, and it should become extensively and permanently established, with its practice ground in the neighbourhood of every large town, and with its periodical contests, it will become an institution of great national importance. Free *swimming-baths* ought to be established in Leeds, and in every large town. Their general introduction would tend to diffuse habits of cleanliness which are almost impossible in the crowded dwellings of the working classes. It would also save many lives, lost from want of a knowledge of the art of swimming.

is now appropriated for the pleasure of a few,
or turned into an inky noisome stream. The
civilization which absorbs so much, should give
somewhat more than it does of the blessed influence
of pure air and light, and free space, to those thousands so long "cabined, cribbed, confined," in miles
of close streets and filthy alleys, that they seem
to have lost almost the consciousness of their depri-
vation.

Some of the proposals in this Essay will no doubt
incur expense; and if looked at without reference
to results, a very large cost. We cannot have
Day Schools, Night Schools, Schools of Science
and Art, Museums, Galleries of Fine Art, without
expense. But the truth remains, that the economy
which counts cost without caring for results, is
as short sighted, and in the end as mistaken, as
it is mean and ungenerous. The wise husbandman
counts not the cost of the seed alone, but the
value of the crop. Look for a moment at the other
side of the account. Calculate the loss which
we sustain in the value of the ignorant workman,
merely as an industrial machine, by inferior skill,
waste of time, and of material. To this large loss,
add that sustained by neglect of the laws of health

and the simplest sanitary conditions, inducing sickness and shortened lives. Add, again, our large poor-rate, which in 99 cases out of 100 is a tax levied by ignorance upon intelligence, of improvidence upon thrift. Add, again, the vast cost of our many charitable institutions, which is another form of poor-rate, but levied with less fairness. Add, again, the cost of the various items of crime, the value of property destroyed, the expenses of law, of the gaol, and of the police, and we shall get a total compared with which tenfold the sum now spent in the education and social improvement of the people would be a mere trifle. Tested by utilitarian views alone, that expenditure which is wisely devoted to the education of the people, to their moral, physical, intellectual, and social improvement, is of all outlays the most economical. An obligation of the strongest kind rests upon each of us to do all he can in the way best suited to his means and capacity, towards ameliorating the social condition of the people amidst whom he dwells. He who attends solely to his personal comforts, or self-advancement, fails not only in the performance of duty, but loses the best cultivation of his own faculties, as well as the purest of sympathetic pleasures. Nor need we set up one form of activity in preference to another. There is, unfortunately, too much need for all. Whether it be in the Ragged School, the Sunday School, the Mechanics' Institute, the Temperance Society, or in any other mode of action calculated to raise his fellow-men, is of secondary consequence : let each one "do the work that lies nearest to him." The main point is, that he does the work he is fitted to do, with singleness of purpose, and "that whatsoever his hand findeth to do, he shall do it *with his might.*"

APPENDICES.

A.—Page 25.

School Certificate.

The following is the School Certificate referred to, and may at least be suggestive to persons desirous to introduce the plan :—

School Certificate of Competency.

First Class.—Reading : History, Bible, &c., with fluency, and precision.

Writing : a prose Essay, slowly read, to be written clearly, and spelt correctly.

Accounts : to Decimal and Vulgar Fractions.

Second Class.—Reading : Bible, well.

Writing : a good small hand.

Accounts : to Proportion.

Third Class.—Reading : simple narratives.

Writing : plainly.

Accounts : the four simple rules.

This   *Class*

School Certificate

Testifies that   , age   years, attended
School at   for   years, and that when   left
it   could Read in   , Write a   ,
Account to   During the time   was
at School   general character was

(Signed)

B.—Page 53.

THE VALUE OF FORTY HOURS.

"Some surprise, and indeed ridicule, has been thrown on the idea of teaching a child to draw by devoting forty hours in the year to it. Forty-eight hours being generally reckoned as two days, the idea of learning anything in forty hours has been at once condemned by unreflecting persons. It would be desirable if persons thinking so would, before all, try to devote forty full and fair hours to the acquirement of some kind of knowledge to which they are as yet strangers; let them even do this in their closet without the aid of a teacher of any kind, but merely following some recognized method of self-instruction; and let them afterwards fairly answer the question whether they have not made real and substantial progress in that time. No person accustomed to exertions, bodily or mental, looks with disdain on forty hours' labour. One hundred and twenty miles seems a long distance to walk, and still a child eight years old could, without any exertion, walk that distance in forty hours on forty consecutive days. In forty hours a man may read Shakspeare through; and if he were to take an hour every week it would be all the better for the reader. A drill serjeant cannot make a perfect soldier in forty hours, but he can make such a difference in the bearing of a recruit as will be evident to the senses of all. Persons profess to teach writing in six lessons of one hour each, and certainly do produce such results that the business is supported by the public."—*First Report of Science and Art*, p. 125.

C.—Page 56.

PROGRESS OF LEEDS MECHANICS' INSTITUTE.

The following table of the members of the Leeds Mechanics' Institute is exclusive of the pupils in the Girls' and Boys' Day Schools; it is also exclusive of the pupils in the School of Art, likewise in connexion with the Institution :—

TABLE OF STATISTICS.

Year.	Life.	Members, 15s.	Subscribers, 15s.	Workmen, 12s.	Youths, 8s.	Ladies. 10s.	Ladies. 5s.	Total.	Ordinary Income.	Number of Pupils in Evening Classes.
1839	...	92	601	166	...	...	...	858	...	140
1840	...	80	560	140	...	...	...	780	...	150
1841	5	77	288	327	...	...	...	697	...	190
1842	5	122	268	191	164	...	...	750	520	200
1843	5	132	248	207	178	...	...	770	520	170
1844	5	123	276	242	226	...	...	872	530	204
1845	4	127	325	361	330	...	34	1181	610	278
1846	4	128	362	412	405	...	104	1415	720	281
1847	4	129	397	439	339	46	187	1541	794	377
1848	4	143	379	455	354	53	176	1564	940	370
1849	4	138	421	466	364	53	195	1641	1006	256
1850	4	146	447	410	273	64	225	1569	961	238
1851	4	149	461	454	285	56	257	1666	1074	238
1852	4	158	525	503	299	81	311	1881	1440	225
1853	5	168	506	498	283	83	329	1872	1190	173
1854	5	172	523	490	315	68	342	1915	1285	243
1855	5	167	488	486	287	54	289	1776	1266	354
1856	5	168	434	429	227	47	231	1541	1220	193
1857	5	173	465	437	204	58	309	1648	1270	185
1858	5	175	448	421	187	41	263	1540	1051	141
1859	7	163	440	498	176	43	221	1548	970	149

D.—Page 57.

CIRCULATION OF BOOKS.

The following is a statement of the Circulation of the Library of the Leeds Mechanics' Institution during the years 1855, 1856, 1857, 1858, and 1859 :—

	No. of Vols.	Per cent.
Theology	7,086	3.10
Philosophy—Education . .	7,210	3.15
Politics—Statistics . . .	1,757	0.75
History—Biography . . .	28,075	12.60
Voyages and Travels . .	11,928	5.35
Poetry—the Drama . . .	7,839	3.45
Fiction	76,779	33.90
Fine Arts—Literature . .	18,358	8.10
Science	8,699	3.85
Natural History—Gardening .	5,580	2.45
Bound Periodicals . . .	22,046	9.72
Unbound ,, . . .	30,725	13.58
	226,082	100.

The following statistics show the proportion of works of fiction during the last fifteen years. They suggest, we think, a strong reason why the class instruction should be much more extended and improved. It would be impracticable and undesirable to force the reading of the members into any particular channel; but surely the facts show all the greater reason why studies of a more solid character should be more encouraged.

Year.	Total Issue of Bound Volumes.	Of which were Fiction	Percentage.
1844	29,458	9,292	31.5
1845	37,137	11,453	30.8
1846	45,467	13,758	30.2
1847	47,349	15,876	33.3
1848	48,918	15,675	32.0
1849	46,014	13,809	30.0
1850	43,279	11,047	25.5
1851	44,847	13,448	27.7
1852	43,206	14,090	32.3
1853	44,424	14,475	32.5
1854	35,936	12,194	33.9
1855	40,890	14,918	36.4
1856	37,936	14,166	37.3
1857	35,449	13,799	38.9
1858	36,831	14,327	38.9
1859	37,784	16,418	43.5

The large increase from 38 per cent. of fiction in 1858, to 43 per cent. in 1859, is due mainly to the introduction of a greater variety of such works from Mudie's Library. And generally it may be noticed that the more instructive works occupy much more time in reading than those of fiction.

D 2.—Page 58.

INDUSTRIAL EDUCATION.

The woollen and worsted manufactures still offer many unsolved problems, in the mechanical and chemical preparation of the fleece for spinning, weaving, finishing, and dyeing. The flax trade—an important staple industry—offers perhaps still greater promise of success, in the removal of foreign or obstructing matters from the fibre, and economizing the mechanism employed in preparing it for and conducting it through the several manufactures in which it is employed. Again, Leeds and its neighbourhood now form a very important centre of the iron trade, both in the production of the raw material from the earth, and in its applications to an infinite variety of purposes. It admits of no dispute, that at every stage of the iron manufacture there is ample scope for the useful exercise of intelligence, founded on a broad basis of real knowledge. When it is considered, too, that in Leeds there are constructed every kind of steam engine, including the railway locomotive; engineering tools, demanding the greatest accuracy and nicest workmanship; every description of spinning and weaving machinery; also many of the automatic fashioning implements now employed for so many purposes: the demand for intellectual qualifications to conduct all these operations successfully and economically, and to keep abreast, if not ahead, of such works elsewhere, is manifestly unlimited.

Some few of the branches of knowledge practically available in connexion with these several trades and manufactures, will define the demand which always must exist, whether or not it is publicly expressed.

1st. A thorough mathematical training and discipline, to enable a man to develop the theory of a machine, to analyse all its working, and to substitute sound reasoning for "rule of thumb" sagacity.

2nd. Mathematics, in relation to the laws of motion and force, and, of course, coupled with geometrical drawing.

3rd. General physics, as being concerned in all machines

and works in which water and air have to be dealt with, and especially the laws of heat—the great motive agent in modern times.

4th. Chemistry is more or less applicable in every branch or stage of manufacture, and it is not improbable that the collateral science of electro-chemistry may also be usefully cultivated.—*W. H. J. Traice.*

E.—Page 61.

SUMMARY *of the* NATURE *and* AMOUNT *of* ASSISTANCE *afforded by the* SCIENCE AND ART DEPARTMENT *to the* INDUSTRIAL CLASSES *in procuring* INSTRUCTION *in* SCIENCE.

I. The Science and Art Department of the Committee of Council on Education aids the industrial classes in procuring instruction in the following sciences:—

1. Practical plane, and descriptive geometry, with mechanical and machine drawing, and building construction.
2. Mechanical physics.
3. Experimental physics.
4. Chemistry.
5. Geology and mineralogy.
6. Natural history, including zoology and botany.

II. The assistance granted by the Science and Art Department is in the form of—

1. Certificate allowances to certified teachers. (See § iii., iv., v., ix.)
2. Payments on results to teachers. (See § x.)
3. Grants towards the purchase of apparatus, books, &c., of schools or classes taught by certified teachers. (See § xii.)
4. Queen's medals and prizes to students, awarded in the annual public local examinations held at all places where there are certificated teachers. (See § vii., viii.) On the results of these examinations the

certificate allowances and payment on results are made to the teachers. (See § ix., x.)

III. Examinations for certificates of competency to teach any of the before-mentioned sciences are held annually by the Science and Art Department, in the first week in November, at South Kensington. Any person whatever may attend this examination by sending in his name to the Secretary of the Science and Art Department, before the 1st October, stating the subject or subjects in which he wishes to be examined. Certificates of three grades are given in each subject. These certificates are only considered as simple *records of the result* of examination in the various sciences before mentioned, entitling the teacher to earn by successful teaching the amounts attached to each, as shown below:—

With a certificate of the 1st grade of competency he is entitled to earn under this head (certificate allowance) £20,

Ditto 2nd grade £15,

Ditto 3rd grade . . . . . . £10.

He is also entitled to earn under the same conditions, (§ ix.), in addition to the above, an amount equal to the value of any certificate of the Education Department which he may hold.

IV. All payments on account of science teaching are made by the Science and Art Department, and are only made when the holder is employed in teaching a school or class not under Inspection by the Education Department, but in connexion with the Science and Art Department.

V. These grants are only made while the teacher is giving instruction in a Day or Evening School or class for the industrial classes (adults or boys above the age of twelve years of age), approved by the Science and Art Department, and open at any time to the visit and Inspection of its officers. Any teacher employed in a Day School under Inspection of the Education Department, must first have obtained the permission of the Education Department to teach in such school or class. This permission is only granted under the conditions of § xiv., xv.

VI. The Science and Art Department requires that suitable premises, with firing, lighting, &c., shall be found and maintained at the cost of the locality where the school or class is held. If at any time the funds do not cover these requisite local expenses, it must be inferred that there is no such demand as the Government is justified in aiding, for instruction in the locality; and the assistance of the Department will be withdrawn.

VII. In order to test the efficiency of the instruction, on the proof of which alone the payments on account of his certificate are made to the teacher, the Science and Art Department holds, in May of each year, a public examination in every locality throughout the United Kingdom where there is a certificated teacher. Application for this examination must be made to the Secretary of the Science and Art Department before the beginning of April in each year, stating the number of persons and the subject or subjects in which they are to be examined. Any persons, whether taught by a certificated master or not, may present themselves at this examination on registering their names in time for the Local Committee to comply with these instructions, and paying a registration fee of not less than 2s. 6d. They are eligible to receive Queen's prizes and Queen's medals.

VIII. The examiners will classify the successful candidates in each subject under the following heads, in lists which will be published:—

1. All those who have passed. The standard of attainment required being low, and only such as will justify the examiner in reporting that the instruction has been sound, and that the students have benefited by it.
2. From among those who have passed, those who have attained a degree of proficiency qualifying them for 1st, 2nd, or 3rd class Queen's prize, as the case may be.
3. The six most successful candidates in each subject, whether taught by a certificated teacher or not, throughout the United Kingdom, if the degree of

proficiency attained be sufficiently high to warrant their being recommended for Queen's medals.

The Queen's prizes consist of books to be chosen by the candidates from lists furnished for that purpose, and are unlimited in number.

The Queen's medals are—one gold, two silver, and three bronze, in each subject for competition throughout the United Kingdom.

IX. The total amount of the pecuniary values attached to the different certificates held by a teacher, both of the Education Department, and of the Science and Art Department (that is, as well for elementary education as for science), being considered a maximum, he receives in respect of it £4 for every student of the industrial classes who passes in any of the before-mentioned subjects of scientific instruction. Provided always, that the amount under this head is never greater than the total amount that the teacher is entitled to earn on account of the certificate or certificates he holds, and that these passed students have received forty lessons at least from him in the year.*

X. And further, the certificated teacher receives for every Queen's prize obtained by his students, a payment in addition of £3, £2, or £1, according to the grade of the Queen's prize.

XI. The claim of a master for the payments under these several heads is made on a form, which will be sent on application. The certificate must be signed by the secretary and chairman of the local class or school; or by at least three of the committee.

XII. A grant towards the purchase of apparatus, fittings, diagrams, &c., of 50 per cent. on the cost of them, is made to Science Schools and classes in Mechanics' and similar

---

* Thus take as an example, a teacher holding—

	£.	s.
1. An Education Department certificate, value	15	0
2. A 2nd grade certificate in inorganic chemistry	7	10
3. A 2nd grade certificate in organic chemistry	7	10
4. A 3rd grade certificate in experimental physics	10	0
Total	£40	0

Institutions where the teacher is certificated. A requisition must in these cases be made.

XIII. Those teachers who are successful in obtaining certificates at the examination in November, at the Science and Art Department, have their expenses paid (second-class railway fare, and 10s. per diem for personal expenses, for every day and night they are required to be in London), on making their application.

XIV. The certificated master of an Elementary School *who has pupil teachers apprenticed to him* cannot receive the science certificate allowance, even if holding a science certificate.

XV. But certificated teachers of Elementary Schools who have not pupil teachers apprenticed to them have their time out of school hours at their own disposal, so far as official regulations are concerned; and may, if further certificated in science, give scientific instruction under the Science and Art Department.

XVI. In order to receive the aid of the Science and Art Department, such instruction must, in accordance with the provisions of §§ iv., v., vi., be given in Mechanics' Institutes, and other places not receiving grants from the Education Department.

XVII. Boys above twelve years of age taught by teachers holding science certificates in Elementary Schools are eligible to be examined for, and to receive Queen's prizes, if successful.

F.—Page 76.

LEEDS EDUCATIONAL BOARD,

For conducting the Oxford University Examinations, the Society of Arts' Examinations, and the Examination for Junior Members of Mechanics' Institutes and Pupils of Night Schools:—

The Worshipful the Mayor of Leeds, WILLIAM KELSALL, Esq.,
President.

Committee.

EDW. BAINES, Esq., M.P.   GEO. S. BEECROFT, Esq., M.P.

The Rev. JAMES ATLAY, D.D., Vicar of Leeds.

The Rev. ALFRED BARRY, B.D., Head Master of the Leeds Grammar School.

Two Representatives of each Institute in Union with the Society of Arts.

At the annual examinations of the Society of Arts, held in London in May last, the following certificates were granted to candidates who had passed the preliminary examinations by the Local Board, appointed by the Leeds Educational Board :—

Arithmetic .	. . 10	Chemistry .	. . 1
Book-keeping	. . 3	English History .	. 1
Algebra .	. . 7	German .	. . 2
Trigonometry	. . 1	Geography .	. . 3
Geometry .	. . 4		

Notwithstanding the comparative success which has thus attended the examinations of the Society of Arts, it must at the same time be evident that the influence of such a stimulus to mental cultivation should be far more widely diffused. There are about ninety Mechanics' Institutes within a reasonable distance of Leeds, besides other Institutes and Evening Schools, which embrace the same class of pupils; and there can be no doubt that if a system of periodical examinations of a lower standard were extended to those who are under the limit fixed by the Society of Arts—sixteen years of age—not only would a much greater number of candidates be gradually prepared for examination in the higher branches of study, but, in addition to these, there are very many who would be induced to use exertions in order to obtain the prizes and certificates offered for the Local Examinations, and so strive more earnestly than they have hitherto done to improve themselves.

At a meeting of the Local Board of Examiners for Leeds, on April 12th, the Rev. J. Atlay, D.D., in the chair, it was

Resolved—"That it is desirable that an examination of the members of Mechanics' and other Institutes, and pupils of Evening Schools under the age of sixteen years, be held

in Leeds during the month of   , and that small
prizes, as well as certificates of three several grades, distinguished as first, second, and third class, be granted in
the following subjects :—

I. Reading.
II. Writing from Dictation.
III. Arithmetic, Four Simple and
        Compound Rules.
IV. Do.   to Decimals.

V. English Grammar.
VI. English History (Period....)
VII. Geography (......)
VIII. Algebra.

"The examinations shall be open to the members of
Mechanics' and other Institutes, and to the pupils of
Evening Schools, the managers of which shall contribute
5s. to the Local Examination Fund for Institutes having
less than 100 members, and schools having less than 100
pupils, and 10s. for those having above that number."

Resolved—"That the carrying out of the foregoing resolution be dependent upon the necessary pecuniary assistance
being received."

The Oxford University Examination Board having con-
sented to the arrangement that the University Local Examinations be conducted by this Board, the names of all
gentlemen on the Oxford Examination Committee have
been added to this Board.

In order to cover the unavoidable expenses of printing,
advertising, prizes, certificates, &c., it is indispensable
that a special fund should be raised for the purpose, and
pecuniary assistance is therefore earnestly solicited. The
execution of the scheme for elementary examinations will
be dependent upon the necessary amount being received;
and for this object only, it is thought desirable that the
subscription from each contributor should not exceed 10s.,
but larger contributions will be received for the general
expenses of the Local Board, or for any of the special
objects of its action.

Subscriptions and donations may be paid to the librarian,
at the Leeds Mechanics' Institution, South-parade.

CHAS. H. COLLIER, M.A., ⎫
BARNETT BLAKE,   ⎬ *Hon. Secretaries.*
JNO. PICKERING,   ⎭

G.—Page 81.—Statistics of Mechanics' and similar Institutions in the Borough of Leeds.

Name of Institution.	Members.		Total.	Rates of Subscription.	Income	Library.		Peri-odicals.	News-papers.	Lec-tures.	No. of Pupils in Classes
	Male.	Fe-male.				No. of Volumes	Issues.				
Beeston	39	2	41	1½d, 2d, and 3d per week.	£28	220	309	7	3	...	30
Bramley	154	8	162	4/ and 5/ per year.	49	950	4,368	9	6	9	30
Chapeltown	227	33	260	4/ and 20/ per year.	100	486	5,256	13	7	21	60
Headingley	76	6	82	2/6, 5/, and 10/ per year.	36	790	1,000	7	9	4	30
Holbeck (Old) . . .	146	14	160	1d and 2d per week.	50	862	1,919	4	8	7	160
Ditto (New) . . .	...	...	554	4/, 6/, 8/, and 10/ per year.	160	1,926	6,260	14	10	8	136
Holbeck and New Wortley	88	3	91	½d and 1d per week.	20	1,439	2,179	8	6	1	77
Hunslet	169	25	194	1/, 1/6, 2/, 2/6 per quarter.	Newly estab-lished.	771	3,000	7	7	7	74
Kirkstall	75	5	80	6/, 8/, 10/ and 21/ per year.	36	870	900	4	6	...	30
Ditto, Educational . .	110	112	222	2/, 4/, 6/, and 10/ per year.	26	940	1,805	10	7	...	206
Woodhouse	187	13	200	1½d, 2d, and 3d per week.	32	670	2,000	8	7	3	140
East Ward	188	12	200	6d and 8d per month.	150	1,500	6,957	12	8	...	40
West-End	100	...	100	6d ⅌ fortnt.; 6/, 10/ ⅌ year.	70	890	...	16	11	4	25
Leeds Young Men's . .	450	...	450	6/, 8/, and 10/ per year.	400	1,200	8,000	35	15	12	90
Leeds Church Institute .	...	...	351	6/, 10/, and 21/ per year.	335	1,780	6,902	24	9	13	12
Catholic Institute . .	88	12	100	5/, 10/, and 15/ per year.	72	1,200	700	9	14	4	...
	2,097	245	3,247		1,564	16,494	51,555	187	123	93	1,140
Leeds Mechanics' Institute	1,284	264	1,548	5/, 8/, 10/, 12/, 15/ per year.	908	10,849	45,895	72	42	28	149
	3,381	509	4,795		2,472	27,343	97,450	259	165	121	1,289

H.—Page 100.

REPORT OF THE LEEDS RAGGED SCHOOLS.

"The Institution was commenced on March 28th, 1859, on which day the first children were received into the school on Richmond-hill. The total number of boys and girls admitted from that period to the end of April last, a period of thirteen months, has been 310, with an average attendance for the last six months of about 80. These have all received instruction in the elementary branches of education, including the knowledge of religious truth, of which most of them were entirely ignorant.

"A mid-day meal is provided, consisting usually of soup and bread.

"About six months after the opening of this school, it was considered desirable to commence a Shoe-black Brigade, and contemporaneously with it a Night Refuge for the boys who were thus to be employed, and for such others as were peculiarly neglected and destitute. The total number of boys received into the Refuge has been 50, and of girls (who are lodged in a separate part of the premises, closely adjoining the master's dwelling) 6. Of the boys who have thus found a home in the Institution, 28 in the whole have been employed as shoe-blacks, and their total earnings for the seven months during which they have been at work, has reached the sum of £79 14s. 10¾d.

"This will appear a large sum, when it is known that the average number of boys thus engaged has only been 10. The highest sum received by any boy in one day (a Saturday) has been 5s. 3d.; in one week, 10s. 8½d. The boys and girls who sleep on the premises receive the whole of their food; and those sent out to labour, either as shoe-blacks or otherwise, their clothing also.

"The number for whom employment has been found in mills, &c., or who have themselves obtained employment, has been, boys, 51; girls, 8:—total, 59. There have been induced to attend other schools, 24; whilst 20 have been required at home by their parents.

"On the other hand, 43 are in the streets again as beggars, or living by dishonesty; and 36, who had their temporary homes in low lodging-houses, have, with their parents, left the town.

"It is important to observe, as fully accounting for these latter statistics, and as having an important bearing upon the whole question of these schools, that out of the number of children received into Richmond-hill School,—to which reference has hitherto been made,—it has been ascertained that no fewer than 53 have either been themselves in prison, or are the children of persons who have been criminally convicted; and that 44 belonged to parents who had no other occupation than that of begging.

"Four months after the opening of the school on Richmond-hill, another school was opened in premises offered to the committee, in Regent-street, Leylands. The number received into this school, since the month of July last, has been 136. Here is no regular Refuge, though 3 girls, who were temporarily destitute, have been taken in to sleep, under the care of the persons who have the charge of the premises; but the whole of the children, who are mostly girls, have their dinners provided,* and are taught reading, &c., along with sewing and knitting.

"The number of names on the books at the end of April last was 75, and the average attendance 56.

"Since the commencement of this school, 10 children have obtained satisfactory employment, and 12 have left in order to attend better schools, chiefly owing to the reformed habits of their parents; the latter most satisfactory result is also to be traced to the good influence of the school.

"It may be added, that not fewer than 22 of the parents of the children attending this school, who had been victims of intemperance, have, through the agency of those connected with the school, been induced to become total abstainers.

"A meeting is held every Wednesday evening for the

---

* The average cost of each child's dinner is rather more than one penny.

mothers of the scholars, at which from 14 to 30 attend; it is conducted by eight ladies, who attend in rotation, and the results have been very encouraging. On Sundays, from 50 to 70 children, consisting of those who belong to the Day School, and a few others out of the neighbourhood, attend, and are instructed by six voluntary teachers.

"The Committee wish to add nothing to the foregoing statement of facts, excepting to express their conviction that the existing provision in these schools meets but the wants of a comparatively small part of the neglected and degraded youthful population of Leeds; and that in whatever aspect Ragged Schools are viewed,—whether with regard to the benefits derived by the poor children themselves, who generally find in these asylums their only means of deliverance from ignorance, debasement, and wretchedness; or in connection with the remarkable diminution of juvenile crime, which is invariably found to follow wherever these schools are established; or whether considered simply as a question of pecuniary gain accruing to the country, by the transference of so many members of the community from the class of the wasteful and the burdensome, to the ranks of the industrious and the helpful,—scarcely any benevolent Institution can have stronger claims upon the support of the public, or call more loudly for extended and persevering effort.

"LEEDS, *May* 21*st*, 1860."

NOTES ON THE RAGGED SCHOOL CHILDREN.

No. 1.—A. B., aged 12 years. I found this boy in one of the lowest brothels in —— street. He was ill in bed at the time. In another bed was a drunken prostitute. She slept on a filthy old mattress, without covering. His mother is dull of hearing. She was said to be always drunk. His father died two months before A. B. was born. His mother lived a life of prostitution afterwards. She was very anxious that we should take her boy, and save him, feeling sure that she was a lost woman without hope. A. B. has often given me deplorable accounts of their wretchedness: was taken by his mother from beerhouse to beerhouse; they were often turned out of bad houses in the middle of the night; had to wander the streets until morning; was often locked up in the house alone while his mother was drinking; was taught by a man to pick the pockets of gentlemen of their handkerchiefs as they passed through the streets; has frequently said that had he not come here he would have been in prison long ago; that if he left the school now he would know better than to do the things he used to do; did not know any better before. When he came to us at first, was almost too weak to walk; was in rags; wore an old coat, which gave him an odd appearance; did not know anything of reading or writing; he was as ignorant and as wretched as possible.

No. 3.—C. D., 12 years old, was born at C——, at which place his father, who was a farmer, died; mother came to Leeds five years since with three boys,—became a drunken prostitute; the boys had to beg and steal for their living, also gathered coals for their mother. I first met with them in —— street; all of them were exceedingly ragged, indeed they had not rags to cover their nakedness. I should think these lads were scarcely ever washed. C. D. had on an old tunic and trousers, with nothing more. He had the appearance of a child just dropping into the grave from want. His habits were filthy, destructive, idle, and vicious,— would gather potato parings in the street and eat them. When he first came to us he ran away three times. Mother was frequently out all night with men, leaving her children at the fireside,—they had no bed to lie down upon. They were often taken to the "Casino." I called upon the mother the Sunday before opening the school; the boys saw me, and ran in to tell their mother; she used horrible language to them, not knowing that I was at the door; she was naked, and sat upon the knees of a low dirty fellow, himself almost naked.

No. 5.—E. F., 13 years old, was born on the high seas; father and mother both died from drunkenness; has one sister almost blind; and has always lived a vagrant life. All the family have been to prison several times for begging and stealing. E. F. lived at the lowest lodging-houses, and relates strange stories of thieves and prostitutes, and knows much of the language peculiar to thieves. "A woman came in one night,—she had picked the pocket of a gentleman of £300 all in notes,—got some silver of the keeper, and took the train the same night for Hull; some time after he saw the woman again in Leeds, dressed like a lady." He can give many cases of a similar nature. E. F., with other lads, paid twopence per night for lodgings. They slept upon wood shavings, with an old sheet thrown over them. A more wretched, filthy-looking lad was never seen. It was with considerable difficulty he was induced to become an inmate; could neither read nor write.

No. 6.—G. H., 11 years old. Father died in the cholera, since which his mother lived the life of a prostitute, and of beastly drunken habits; for years has had no home for her children; has four boys. G. H. and I. J. have frequently been to prison.

I. J. is now in gaol, and at the expiration of his imprisonment will be committed to the Reformatory for five years. These four lads, with their mother, lodged in a cellar-dwelling with Wm. Y.'s mother, who is also of the same character; Mrs. Y. had two boys : all these, with the men they lived with, slept in the same den; had no beds to lie upon, got a quantity of straw, and were covered with their old rags. I think it would be difficult to meet with more wretchedness and vice.

No. 7.—K. L., 11 years old, has parents, both of whom have been frequently to prison; home most wretched; no bed to lie upon; often called to see them when the children were at the fireside, with not an article of clothing to cover their nakedness. In all respects K. L. was growing up like his parents, and stole anything from them he could. They ill-used him, making him both black and blue; confining him for days together; stripped him naked; often would not allow him anything to eat; locked him in the house, he got out of the window, and ran into the streets naked. Young as he was, he was the ringleader of eight or ten young thieves; got them to steal for him, promising to let them join with him; if they would not, he beat them; frequently did not get home till midnight; parents were often sleeping, and said nothing to him; when out at night with other lads, threw stones at people's windows, destroying them; was very fond of dogs; was constantly taking dogs home; was at the last Holbeck feast, stealing articles from the stalls and picking pockets; was admitted an inmate of the Dormitory at the School the same week. Father said that he was completely mastered, and that they could do nothing with him. When I told him that we would take him off their hands, they scarcely knew how to express their pleasure.

No. 14.—M. N., aged 14 years; parents lived at Leeds; father been married three times, and is footman to Mr. O. This boy came to us a few weeks since in a very destitute condition; had been living in lodging-houses in —— street, &c.; told me part of his history; and the day following I made out his parents, and learned the following particulars : That he had acquired very bad habits, and had been taken to prison for stealing money from his master. On one occasion he stole a bunch of keys, and was detected before he got to the money drawer; another time he got six shillings in copper; often stole money from his father's pockets when asleep; got his stepmother's gold ring, with other articles. His mother was very injudicious in her treatment of him; frequently told him that he would go to the gallows. On one occasion she gave him a practical illustration of what hanging would be, by putting his father's scarf round his neck, and giving him a "good twitch, until he was black in the face;" when she released him, she reminded him that they would not set him at liberty as she had done. When he stole her ring, with other articles, she threatened him that if he did not bring them back at noon she would "cut his head clean off."

M. N. did not return for execution. They heard no more of him for three months, until I informed them where he was. When I spoke to the father about him, he "did not care where he was, nor what became of him; would be glad if he were dead; mattered not to him whether we took him or not; had entirely disowned him, and would have nothing more to do with him."

No. 27.—P. Q., aged 13 years; father dead,—mother an Irish Protestant. P. Q. kept company with some noted young thieves; mother could not get him to work; she had him before the magistrates three times, wishing them to deal with him; she abused him as a coward for not stealing, so as to be apprehended and sent to a Reformatory. They have a very wretched home. I have thought this lad's case was hopeless.

I.—Page 102.

Extracts from the Code of the Committee of Council on Education.

Ragged Schools.

"Ragged Schools are schools voluntarily established and maintained for children who have no home, or no reputable home, and who depend upon school for domestic and industrial, as well as for literary, instruction; but who attend without legal compulsion, and are vagrant rather than criminal.

"Ragged Schools must fulfil the following conditions:—

"*(a).* The title of Ragged School, or some other equivalent name, must be retained.

"*(b.)* Both literary and industrial instruction must be given.

"*(c).* No fees must be received.

"*(d).* Accurate accounts must be kept of all receipts and expenditure; and if the managers attempt other objects besides the daily instruction of children, the expenditure upon such other objects, and upon instruction, must be separately stated.

"*(e).* The managers must certify, and the Inspector must report, that adequate means are taken to confine the children attending the school to that class which cannot be associated with the children of respectable labouring men; that reading, writing, and arithmetic (as far as the first four rules, simple and compound), are well taught in the school; and that its discipline and moral influence are such as are calculated to benefit the special class of scholars.

"Grants for building Ragged Schools, also for books, maps, and diagrams, are made.

"Ragged Schools may receive annual grants equal per annum to—

"(a). One-half of the rent of the premises in which industrial instruction is carried on.

"(b). One-third of the cost of tools and of raw material for labour.

"(c). Five shillings per annum per industrial scholar, according to the average number under industrial instruction throughout the year preceding the date of Inspection.

"(d). The ordinary rate in augmentation of any certificated teacher's salary."

CERTIFIED INDUSTRIAL SCHOOLS.

"Schools of the character described in the last section, in England and Wales, may be certified by the Committee of Council on Education, pursuant to Acts of Parliament 17 & 18 Vict. c. 74, 18 & 19 Vict. c. 28, and 20 & 21 Vict. c. 48.

"The managers of schools thus sanctioned or certified, acquire power to detain and recapture all such children as they agree to receive under magisterial sentence.

"The persons liable to magisterial sentence under these Acts are—

"*In England and Wales*, children apparently under fourteen and over seven years of age, who are taken into custody on a charge of vagrancy: that is—

"(a). Begging; or,

"*(b)*. Wandering, without any home or settled place of abode, or proper guardianship, and without any lawful or visible means of subsistence.

"The managers may recover the cost of such children while in their custody—

"*In England and Wales*, from the parents, at a rate not exceeding 3*s*. per week. (Act 20 & 21 Vict. c. 48, s. 15.)

"Schools so certified may receive, from the money voted by Parliament for public education, in addition to the above grants, the sum of 6*d*. per day, up to a maximum of £7 10*s*. per annum, for every child admitted into the establishment under magisterial sentence.

"Grants for building schools intended to be certified, are made at a rate not exceeding £30 per inmate. A dormitory and all other proper appliances must be provided for the lodging and instruction of each inmate, in respect of whom such a grant is made."

It has been contended that the above assistance is not adequate to the exigencies of Ragged and Industrial Schools. Whatever truth there may be in this view in some places, it is scarcely applicable to Leeds, where no advantage has yet been taken of the above provisions. With the aid of the State fully invoked, and the assistance of private benevolence, there would appear to be sufficient means to supply the educational need of the ragged, outcast, or neglected children of Leeds.

J.—Page 109.

The following is the CIRCULATION of PERIODICALS and
NEWSPAPERS in LEEDS, May, 1860, as collected by
Mr. J. PICKERING, Secretary to the Leeds Mechanics'
Institute :—

LITERARY.	Weekly.	Monthly.
All the Year Round	439	117
Annals of Leeds	1,011	...
Beeton's Dictionary of Information . .	...	413
,, Household Management . .	...	163
Boys' Own Magazine	...	331
British Controversialist . . .	...	20
Builder (The)	51	...
Cassell's Family Paper . . .	3,046	...
,, History of England . .	837	...
,, Natural History . . .	...	237
Chambers's Journal	264	220
,, Encyclopædia . . .	292	107
Companion for Youth	...	67
Cornhill Magazine	...	700
Dictionary of Daily Wants . .	...	654
,, of Useful Knowledge . .	...	114
Englishwoman's Domestic Magazine . .	...	354
Family Economist	108	...
,, Herald	2,834	62
Gardeners' Weekly Magazine . . .	33	...
Home Magazine	567	...
Ladies' Treasury	...	112
Leisure Hour	611	363
Leeds Herald	...	2,000
London Journal	4,234	...
Macmillan's Magazine	...	106
Miscellaneous Novels, in weekly parts, published by Reynolds, Lea, and Lloyd	2,234	39
Musical Times	...	140
Once a Week	194	43
Pastime	...	12
Popular Lecturer	...	9
Reasoner (The)	31	...
Reynolds' Miscellany	2,809	...
Welcome Guest	132	...
Young England's Newspaper . . .	...	71
Total . .	19,727	6,454

RELIGIOUS.	Weekly.	Monthly.
Appeal (The)	...	240
Baptist Magazine	...	31
,, Messenger	...	239
Bible Class Magazine	...	185
Biblical Treasury	...	101
Book (The) and its Mission . . .	...	42
British Messenger	...	156
Cassell's Bible	1,248	112
Child's Companion	...	778
,, Own Magazine	...	313
Children's Friend	...	21
,, Magazine	...	29
Christian Cabinet	14	...
,, Miscellany	...	539
,, Treasury	...	98
,, Spectator	...	31
,, Witness	...	81
,, World	...	28
Christian's Penny Magazine . . .	...	129
Church Missionary Gleaner . . .	...	14
,, Missionary Instructor . . .	...	196
,, Missionary Intelligencer . .	...	31
,, of England Magazine . . .	...	33
,, (The)	...	301
Churchman's Penny Magazine . . .	...	279
Dewdrop (The)	...	40
Early Days	...	423
Ensign (The)	46	...
Evangelical Magazine	...	69
Family Treasury	...	183
Friendly Visitor	...	21
Good Words	...	139
Gospel Missionary	...	87
,, Standard	...	18
,, Trumpet	...	69
Jewish Herald	...	11
Juvenile Instructor	...	96
,, Missionary Herald . . .	...	77
,, Missionary Magazine . . .	...	88
Lamp of Love	...	85
Mother's Friend	...	247
New Park Street Pulpit	...	13
Notes on Scripture Lessons . . .	...	488
Penny Post	...	94
Revival (The)	176	...
Sabbath School Messenger . . .	...	47
Sunday at Home	619	338
Carried forward . .	2,103	6,640

RELIGIOUS.	Weekly.	Monthly.
Brought forward . .	2,103	6,640
Sunday School Penny Companion . .	...	29
,, Penny Magazine . .	...	48
,, Times	272	...
,, Union Magazine . .	...	118
Tract Magazine	...	210
Wesleyan Magazine	...	295
,, Sunday School Magazine . .	...	378
Yorkshire Pulpit	...	250
Total .	2,375	7,968

TEMPERANCE.		
Adviser (The)	...	300
Alliance (The)	374	...
Band of Hope	...	5,273
British Workman	...	7,185
Spectator (The)	...	33
Temperance Advocate	...	211
,, Tracts	...	1,670
Total .	374	14,672

NEWSPAPERS.	Daily.	Weekly.
Bell's Life	...	558
Daily News	13	...
,, Telegraph	75	...
Era (The)	...	51
Field (The)	...	39
Illustrated London News	...	320
,, Times	...	212
Leeds Mercury, Times, and Intelligencer, together	...	11,000
Leeds Express	...	8,508
Manchester Examiner and Times . .	1,302	...
,, Guardian	800	...
Morning Herald	7	...
,, Post	6	...
,, Star	86	...
Punch	...	470
Sporting Life	...	1,394
,, Telegraph	...	230
Standard	128	...
Sun	4	...
Times	119	...
Weekly Dispatch	...	110
,, Times, News of the World, and Reynolds' Newspaper . . .	...	2,045
Total . .	2,540	24,937

K.—Page 111.

CLASSIFICATION OF TRADES OF THE DEPOSITORS IN THE
LEEDS, SKYRAC, AND MORLEY SAVINGS BANK.

Description of Depositors.	Male.	Female	Total.
Bookbinders, Printers, &c. . .	111	...	111
Book-keepers, Shopmen and women, Warehousemen, &c. . .	500	2	502
Colliers, Miners, Delvers, &c. . .	225	...	225
Cotton, Linen, Silk, and Stuff Trades	209	74	283
Domestic Servants	261	1,728	1,989
Joiners, Coachmakers, &c. . .	438	...	438
Leather Trade, Saddlers, &c. . .	154	...	154
Lodging House Keepers, Widows, Spinsters, and Married Women	...	713	713
Masons and Bricklayers . . .	582	...	582
Mechanics and Iron Workers . .	924	5	929
Milliners, Dressmakers, and Needle-women	...	322	322
Minors	1,165	1,042	2,207
Other Trades, not particularly specified	512	38	550
Painters, Plumbers, Gas and Glass Makers, &c. . . .	133	...	133
Policemen, Soldiers, and Cab-drivers	191	...	191
Schoolmasters and Artists . .	156	127	283
Shoemakers, Tailors, and Hatters .	302	...	302
Shopkeepers, Beersellers, Hawkers, &c.	479	72	551
Small Farmers, Gardeners, &c. .	446	...	446
Trust Accounts, and Friendly and Charitable Societies . -	...	...	467
Woollen Trade, Dyers, &c. . .	1,356	144	1,500
Nov. 20*th*, 1859.—Total . . .	8,144	4,267	12,878

L.—Page 112.

CONDITIONS AND ADVANTAGES OF THE BRANCHES OF THE
WEST-RIDING OF YORKSHIRE PENNY SAVINGS BANK.

It is required by the Central Committee of the West-Riding of Yorkshire Penny Savings Bank, that those who intend to establish a Branch in connexion therewith, shall form a committee, consisting of a president, actuary, auditor, and as many committee-men as will be sufficient, efficiently and conveniently, to work the Branch Bank. The Branch should be open at least weekly, at such hour as may be most convenient for depositors. The actuary, and two other members of the Branch committee, must be present at each meeting. The actuary should remit all the deposits received by him to the Central Bank, or to the District treasurer where one has been appointed, immediately after the receipt thereof. The books, checks, returns, and forms, provided by the Central Bank, should be the only ones used in the business of Branches.

The whole business of a Branch Bank need not take more than one hour and a half in each week.

These regulations being attended to by the Branch Bank, the advantage it receives from the Central Bank are,—a guarantee for the safety of all deposits as soon as they are received by the treasurer of the Central Bank;—a regular check and audit of the accounts of the Branch;—interest to the depositors of three per cent. upon each sum of one or more pounds deposited for every whole month during which it is deposited;—an allowance of one-half per cent. upon the balance which stands to the credit of the Branch Bank at the Central Bank on the 31st of December in each year;— an annual audit, by which every depositor can check the amount of his own deposit, without that deposit being known as to its amount to any other depositor. The Rules are certified under Government. Depositors may, without expense or trouble, transfer their deposits from one Branch to another, as they may change their places of abode.

Further information, and the necessary forms of account, may be obtained at the office of the West-Riding Bank, No. 2, East-parade, Leeds.

M.—Page 113.

WORKSHOP SAVINGS BANKS AND SICK SOCIETIES.

A practical illustration of a Savings Bank and Friendly Society in connexion with the place of employment, is furnished at the Victoria Foundry, Leeds, employing about 450 men and boys. Each workman who wishes to deposit in the Bank, informs the time-keeper, before the wages are

paid, what amount he wishes to invest, and it is deducted
from his wages. The average number of depositors is about
50; and during the three years and a half that the plan has
been in operation, they have

Deposited	£490
Withdrawn	262

Balance now (June, 1860) in the Bank . £228

Five per cent. interest is given to the depositors by the
employers.

The Sick Society consists of 95 men and boys, the former
of whom pay 3d. weekly, and the latter 1½d. The men
receive 8s. per week, and the boys 4s. per week, in sickness.
The wife of a member receives £5 on his death, and £3 is
paid on the death of a wife. During two years and a half
that the Sick Society has existed, about £140 has been paid
in allowance for sickness and at death. Both the Bank and
the Sick Society are conducted by the men themselves,
quite independent of the firm.

At the works of Messrs. Kitson & Co., Airedale Foundry,
all the workpeople (about 1,000) are required to belong to the
Provident Sick Society in connexion with the works. The
Society is managed by a committee of five,—viz., two fore-
men and three workmen,—who decide upon all cases of
relief. A member entitled to relief receives one-third of his
regular wages during sickness; and in case of his death, a
sum equal to four full weeks' wages is paid to assist in
defraying the funeral expenses. The most novel feature of
this Society is the method of contribution. All the hands
are required to work ten minutes per day, equal to an hour
per week, above the regular time. The value of this labour
is placed to the credit of the sick fund. The Society was
established in 1852, and some conception may be formed of
the amount of good accomplished by it, from the fact, that
the amount paid from January, 1852, to June, 1860, in

Sick relief, was . . .	£2,529	3 0
Payments at death (60 deaths)	221	2 10

£2,750 5 10

The above is exclusive of the amount paid to the surgeon
for medical attendance. The advantages of such a Sick
Society over the ordinary ones are considerable. There is
no trouble or expense in collecting. There are no public-

house expenses or temptations. As the members know each other, the frauds from feigned sickness, and in other ways, are much more difficult, in fact almost impossible.

N.—Page 119.

ATTENDANCE AT CHEAP CONCERTS.

RATIONAL RECREATION SOCIETY.—MUSIC HALL.				
Seasons.	Front Seats.	Saloon.	Gallery.	Total.
1853	5,156	7,953	3,534	16,643
1854	6,754	8,133	4,140	19,027
1855	3,651	3,359	2,138	9,148
1856	4,148	5,092	3,013	12,253
1857	6,309	7,678	4,278	18,265
1858	4,617	5,875	3,748	14,240
Total	30,635	38,090	20,851	89,576

TOWN HALL CONCERT SOCIETY.—TOWN HALL.				
Seasons.	Front Seats.	Second Seats.	Promenade.	Total.
1859	7,405	9,893	10,299	27,597
1860	13,162	9,618	9,416	32,196
Total	20,567	19,511	19,715	59,793